Routledge Revivals

The Kingdom of Toro in Uganda

First published in 1975, *The Kingdom of Toro in Uganda* describes the foundation of the Toro kingdom in the nineteenth century by the rebel prince Kaboyo, and investigates how Kasagama, Kaboyo's grandson, was able to recreate, with little local support, a kingdom far more extensive than Kaboyo had ever envisaged. His personal authority was established by his insistence that its roots were traditional, thus satisfying the requirements of 'indirect rules' at a time when this ill-defined concept served both as the shibboleth and the escape clause for an overstretched British colonial administration. Although Kasagama's son, Rukidi, was able to combine authority with personal popularity and to take advantage of colonial innovations without losing control of his kingdom, the ending of colonial rule brought an end to Toro as he knew it. In an independent Uganda the particularism stressed by Toro's rulers could not survive. This book will be of interest to students of history, colonialism, African studies and ethnic studies.

The Kingdom of Toro in Uganda

Kenneth Ingham

Routledge
Taylor & Francis Group

First published in 1975
By Methuen & Co Ltd

This edition first published in 2023 by Routledge
4 Park Square, Milton Park, Abingdon, Oxon, OX14 4RN
and by Routledge
605 Third Avenue, New York, NY 10017

Routledge is an imprint of the Taylor & Francis Group, an informa business

A Library of Congress record exists under ISBN: 0416802001

ISBN: 978-1-032-61252-2 (hbk)
ISBN: 978-1-003-46276-7 (ebk)
ISBN: 978-1-032-61260-7 (pbk)

Book DOI 10.4324/9781003462767

KENNETH INGHAM

THE KINGDOM OF TORO IN UGANDA

METHUEN & CO LTD
11 New Fetter Lane · London EC4

First published 1975 by Methuen & Co Ltd

Printed in Great Britain by
Richard Clay (The Chaucer Press) Ltd,
Bungay, Suffolk

ISBN 0 416 80200 1 hardback
ISBN 0 416 80210 9 paperback

Distributed in the USA by
HARPER & ROW PUBLISHERS, INC.
BARNES & NOBLE IMPORT DIVISION

Contents

Preface

Behind much of the writing of African history there lurks the knowledge that today there exist in Tropical Africa many large, new, independent states, while in Southern Africa black majorities are still ruled by white minority governments. This knowledge often affects the form in which the history of Africa is presented, converting it into a morality play in which the achievement of African independence becomes the goal of the pilgrim's progress. Contemporary African political leaders are all too aware that independence holds no such finality, determined though they may be to assist their fellow Africans in the southern part of the continent in their efforts to escape white domination. For the historian it is a particularly dangerous misinterpretation because it diverts his attention from the particular to the general, from the study of individuals and individual societies to the obsession with race.

In writing the history of Toro such an approach is particularly confusing. Until very recently neither the rulers nor the people were concerned with Uganda as a whole, or even with independence in the special sense of ending European colonialism. If one wishes to seek insights into the history of Toro it is better to look for them in a very different context. The Nilotic incursions into the Empire of the Bacwezi, for example, might well find a parallel in the Saxon invasion of Romanized Britain, while the Rwenzururu movement, though it took place only recently, was not dissimilar from the British resistance to the Saxons in the mountains of Wales. Kasagama, too, struggling to assert his sovereignty against the encroachments of the Protectorate Administration and trying to distinguish what was essential to Toro and what might, if necessary, be surrendered, was not unlike Henry II of England, striving to resolve the sovereignties of Church and State. To make any of these comparisons is not to associate Toro irrevocably with any one period of British history, or indeed of the history of any country. It simply emphasizes the links which bind humanity together and helps to dispel the idea that there is any mystique about the history of Africa.

In writing this book I have tried to use as extensively as possible the normal tools of the historian – documents, reports, memoirs and other written source material. These, it is true, concentrate the attention upon government and governors, rather than upon the people as a whole. Yet they do not distort the story completely. Such oral evidence as I have had, from a wide range of sources, confirms the central role of the monarchy throughout the kingdom's existence. I am deeply indebted to my informants, many of them very old friends, and if I have misrepresented the evidence they gave the fault is entirely my own. To the British Academy, too, I am most grateful, for the award of a visiting fellowship which enabled me to revisit Uganda after a ten years' absence in order to work in the National Archives, to travel again to the Mountains of the Moon and to meet people I had known so well during the years I spent at Makerere. The cooperation of the Uganda Government in granting me access to the archives and the guidance so generously given by the staff in Entebbe were of the greatest help to me and I am glad of the opportunity to express my appreciation. In London the staffs of the Public Record Office and of the library and archives of the Church Missionary Society were courteous and helpful as they seem invariably to be. A special word should be said about Mr Oliver Furley, late of Makerere University and now at Lanchester Polytechnic. His two articles on Kasagama which appeared in the *Uganda Journal* are the starting point for anyone interested in studying the history of the revival of Toro. By their organization and hospitality Mr and Mrs Furley also contributed immeasurably to the success of my most recent visit to Uganda and I am also grateful to the authorities of Makerere University and to the staff of the History Department for all the help they gave me. Mr J. B. Kaboha, of the Commonwealth Secretariat, has been my mentor in regard to so many aspects of my subject that I cannot easily estimate the extent of my indebtedness to him. I can only hope that he will forgive any errors of fact or of interpretation which may appear in this book.

The task of typing the manuscript almost literally fell upon Mrs P. Roberts and Mrs M. D. Battson, secretaries in the History Department who, year by year, survive the rigours of their work with unfailing kindness and good humour. I owe them a great debt of gratitude.

And finally to my wife, companion alike in my travels and researches, I owe the completion of this book. Stimulus, critic and helpmeet, she précised documents, typed notes and early drafts of the text, and provided the sort of hospitality which made new friends in Uganda as well as strengthening old ties. As always it is to her that I owe most, and I am happy to record my debt.

Bristol May 1974 KENNETH INGHAM

Glossary of Vernacular Terms in Frequent Use

State	*Language*	*Inhabitants*	
		Singular	*Plural*
Buganda	Luganda	Muganda	Baganda
Busongora			Basongora
Bunyoro	Runyoro	Munyoro	Banyoro
Bwamba			Baamba
		Mukonjo	Bakonjo
Nkore (pre-Colonial) / Ankole (Colonial)	Runyankore	Munyankore	Banyankore
Toro	Rutoro	Mutoro	Batoro

To avoid further complexity several of these nouns are used adjectivally in the text.

The Empire of Bunyoro-Kitara

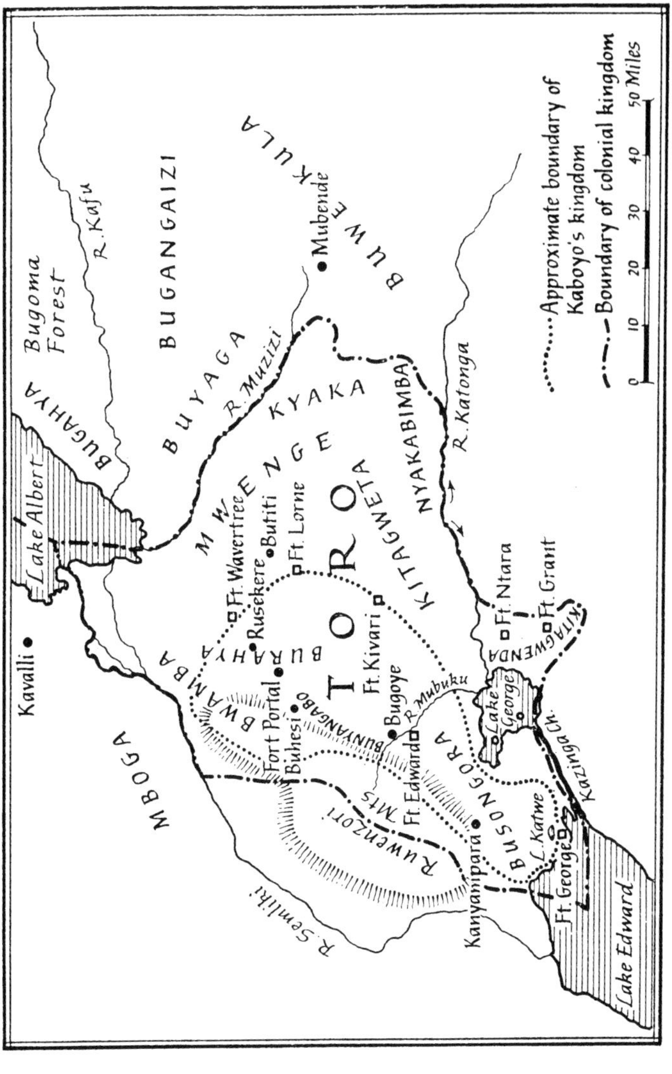

The Toro Kingdom

Introduction · Imperial Origins

This book is not so much the story of a people as the history of a state. The Kingdom of Toro in western Uganda was created as a monarchy. After a brief extinction it was revived because another monarch was available. When monarchies were abolished in Uganda in 1967 Toro ceased to exist. The people of Toro were initially bound together less by a sense of national unity than by a localized desire to escape the pressures arising from membership of a larger empire and their subordination to what they regarded as a remote and arbitrary government. Subsequently it was the monarchy which supplied the cohesive force, and in the last resort the monarchy and the kingdom fell before the might of a new and larger state. The history of Toro is, therefore, the story of the struggle for sovereignty, and although economic and social changes were to exert their influence, constitutional conflict and political manoeuvre must remain at the heart of the narrative.

At its widest extent, in the first half of the twentieth century, the kingdom covered an area of about 5500 square miles. Triangular in shape, one of its boundaries lay along the snowy crest of the Ruwenzori Mountains, referred to by writers from the time of the ancient Greeks as the Mountains of the Moon. The two other sides jutted eastward between the kingdoms of Buganda to the north and Ankole to the south. Within these frontiers lay some of the most beautiful and most fertile land in one of the richest regions to be found in Africa. From the grasslands of the Busongora plain in the south-west, teeming with cattle until rinderpest wiped out the herds towards the close of the nineteenth century, to the rolling hills of Mwenge in the north, the country was a paradise for pastoralists. The eastern foothills of the Ruwenzoris, blessed with a reliable rainfall and with their crater lakes, natural storage tanks to supply both men and beasts, were ideal for agriculture and cattle grazing alike. The uplands to the east of Lake George responded readily to cultivation and produced large quantities of food – millet, beans, sweet potatoes and plantains – while Lake Katwe in southern Busongora, and formerly Lake Kasese, too, produced salt in quantities large enough to supply the needs of all south-western Uganda.

The people who inhabited this prosperous region were as richly varied as the country itself. The Baamba living in the forests on the northern mountain slopes had a close affinity with the forest dwellers of the upper Congo to the west. In their tiny, single-street villages, without even a headman, their strongest ties were those of lineage and clan. Armed with bows and arrows they hunted for food and were beginning to till the soil with primitive tools. Along the lower slopes of the eastern and southern Ruwenzoris and spreading out from the foothills to the plains beyond, the Bakonjo, short, dark and stocky men, preferred the open country where they could cultivate the soil without the labour of destroying the forest; but under pressure they did not hesitate to retreat up the mountainside and there to open up the undergrowth in order to grow their crops. Their diet was mainly millet with peas and beans. They had no cattle and their only stock were sheep and goats. Culturally they formed a bridge between the forest dwellers to the west and the Bantu of the lake regions to the south and east, though in the late nineteenth century circumstances forced them into a closer association with the Baamba. In Busongora they had for centuries intermingled with bands of pastoralists while remaining culturally distinct from them. These latter, as European travellers were frequently to observe with wonder, differed markedly from their Bantu neighbours in physical appearance as well as in the conduct of their lives. Tall, spare, finely featured and pale in complexion, their whole being, their ritual and their routine, centred round their cattle. They dominated the open plain to the north of Lake Edward, leaving the Bakonjo to pursue their existence in scattered pockets of cultivated land in their midst or to concentrate among the crater lakes and foothills of the Ruwenzoris.

The remainder of the country, stretching eastward almost as far as the mysterious hill of Mubende, was the home of a mixed pastoralist and agricultural population. Although the former claimed an aristocratic superiority there was much intermarriage and clear-cut ethnic lines were often hard to draw in spite of the complicated genealogical trees concocted by the ruling families to emphasize their status. Because traditional authority had its centre to the east, beyond the boundaries of colonial Toro, individualists, malcontents, adventurers and all who sought to escape too close a contact with their rulers, tended to drift westward to the region east of the Ruwenzoris which became known as Toro and gave its name to the whole kingdom. They were men of many clans yet having much in common so far as culture and tradition were concerned. Most were agriculturalists and the temptation to enjoy the fine agricultural land proved an added incentive to them to quit the domination of the pastoralists. They left behind them in Mwenge and Kyaka men of a more conformist disposition who accepted overlords who were themselves content to exercise their authority in accordance with directives from their own master, the ruler of the Empire of Kitara.

That these diverse peoples should have been brought together under one ruler owes much to the traditions of Kitara. The Kingdom of Toro existed first, embryonically and precariously, for some fifty years in the middle of the nineteenth century and was extinguished in the late 1870s. It revived some ten or a dozen years later due to the initiative of an adventurous Englishman and the opportunism of the son of a former ruler. Taking advantage of the protection offered by Britain, two successive rulers, ambitious and assertive and endowed with powerful personalities, enveloped themselves in an aura of neo-traditional authority and surrounded their kingdom with the sanctity of a pseudo antiquity. British administrators, many of them fervent exponents of indirect rule, came to accept this version of Toro's past and gave it their support. But ultimately the very success of the two rulers was to be the kingdom's undoing. In an independent Uganda the persistence of what looked like local power pockets was deemed unacceptable and Toro, along with its more genuinely ancient and more wilfully powerful neighbour, Buganda, was abolished in 1967.

The origins of the kingdom formed a natural part of the kaleidoscopic history of the lake region of central Africa, and but for British intervention Toro would almost certainly have vanished as quickly as it emerged, like other presumptuous princedoms reabsorbed into the background from which they sprang. Toro's own background is to be sought in the traditions of two successive empires, that of the Bacwezi (sing. Mucwezi) in the fifteenth century, and the later empire of the Babito (sing. Mubito). Of the earlier empire, Kitara, little is known with certainty either as to its extent or its character. Both these questions have given rise to considerable conjecture, with fantasy pressing hard upon fact, for the Bacwezi have left a reputation which has in no way declined with the passing years and which rests upon the belief that in their heyday they possessed outstanding qualities.

Without belittling the achievements of these early empire builders scholars have attempted to evaluate the small amount of evidence available about them and certain conclusions seem reasonably firm. The Bacwezi would appear to have been members of a ruling pastoralist clan, one of many similar clans collectively referred to in Uganda as Bahima (sing. Muhima), the forefathers of, among others, the pastoralists of nineteenth-century Busongora. Not all their subjects were of a similar strain, for in areas better suited to agriculture a darker race of

Bantu was to be found, and the two cultures helped to sustain each other in spite of the distinctions upon which the pastoralists tried to insist.

The remains of large capital cities like the one at Bigo on the Katonga River suggest that the ruling dynasty lived in some splendour, sustained by substantial tribute, yet it is tempting to assume that their system of government was not highly developed. Dr Karugire, in his scholarly study of the Nkore Kingdom, concludes that the effective influence of the Bacwezi extended only to Bwera and Nkore, although according to oral tradition Wamara, the last of the Bacwezi rulers, posted governors in more outlying districts of his empire.[1] It is not, however, improbable that groups of pastoralists, accustomed to seasonal migration, owed their more direct allegiance to clan leaders and, although paying tribute, offered only a remote loyalty to the ruling dynasty and its local representatives.

Just as it is difficult to establish a clear-cut estimate of the rulers' authority, so too is it impossible to discover any sharply defined imperial boundary. Such restriction would in any case have appeared irksome to a predominantly pastoral society. At their furthest extent, therefore, the dominions of the Bacwezi may have stretched from the southern slopes of the Ruwenzoris in the west to the Kagera River in the south and the shores of Lake Victoria in the east, with their northern limits somewhere between Lake Albert and Lake Kyoga. Over that area, however, the power and even the influence of the Bacwezi varied greatly in intensity.

It is possible that the whole of what was later to become the Kingdom of Toro fell within the Bacwezi empire at its widest extent, although in view of its varied population it was unlikely to have constituted in any sense a political unit or even an administrative subdivision. For an example of independent action on the part of some of the inhabitants of this area one may turn to Sir Apolo Kaggwa's account of how, about the time of the collapse of Bacwezi suzerainty, one clan group migrated from Busongora with their herds and halted for a time som ninety miles to the east, in Bwera, before finally settling a further thirty miles from their starting point, in the modern county of Gomba.[2]

Striking though the rule of the Bacwezi appears to have been its duration was short, while its speedy collapse, whether in response to internal or external pressures, gives some support to the view that its substance was slight. Dr Karugire[3] and Professor Kiwanuka,[4] for example, argue that Bacwezi domination lasted for only two generations. Several writers have attributed its downfall to the invasion of the empire by Nilotic conquerors from the north.[5] Kiwanuka, however, has challenged this theory, suggesting instead that the power of the Bacwezi disintegrated due to internal weakness and that the arrival of the invaders, coinciding as it did with changes which were already under way, only contributed marginally to the overthrow of the dynasty. His argument is based upon his own interpretation of the chronology of events in the neighbouring kingdom of Buganda and is supported by the surprisingly small cultural impact made by the invaders who adopted the language and many of the customs of the people whom they came to rule.[6] Professor Oliver had earlier suggested that this latter phenomenon was most probably due to a sense of cultural inferiority on the part of the newcomers and there are certainly examples of such behaviour in other parts of the world at different times. Uncertainty, therefore, remains on this issue. There is, however, a tradition among the Batoro that the disappearance of the Bacwezi is characterized by the word *emigayo* (contempt), the implication being that the charisma which had formerly attached to the Bacwezi was dispelled when their subjects recognized their human weakness.[7] An interesting parallel, and possibly the only one, occurred recently when the commoner president of Uganda, Milton Obote, overthrew the ruler of Toro in 1967, and the word *emigayo* was once again employed to describe what had happened.

The importance of Kiwanuka's thesis, however, is that it demands an investigation of the easy assumption that the Nilotic Babito dynasty simply took over from the Bacwezi an extensive empire in working order. If one compares the various oral traditions upon which any reconstruction of the origins and character of the new hegemony must be built, it seems clear that whatever form of rule was introduced it had to be created almost *de novo*. The invaders, however numerous their original stock, probably penetrated in large numbers only into the northern part of what is now Bunyoro. Small groups then moved further south into the area of Bacwezi authority where their initial influence seems to have been based upon opportunism and a natural aggressiveness rather than upon weight of numbers. Nor is it wholly out of the question that at some stage in their migration, even before they reached the heart of the empire, some of the Babito married into the Bacwezi clan although the circumstances of the marriages probably differed from those related in the traditions of Bunyoro. Subsequently the Babito laid great stress upon their family links with the Bacwezi to justify their assumption of power to the extent that, although they were not pastoralists when they reached Bwera, they rapidly accustomed themselves to this role and embodied the rituals associated with cattle-keeping in their own symbolism of monarchy as proof of their Bacwezi descent.

The assumption of these outward trappings of Bacwezi authority, accompanied though they were by the frequently repeated claim to hereditary succession and the adoption of the title *Mukama* (pl. *Bakama*) by the head of the clan, was not of itself enough to establish the Babito as unchallenged rulers of Kitara. It seems likely, for example, that they found it necessary to enlist the support of some of the inhabitants of the empire by associating members of some of their leading clans with the ritual of monarchy – as keepers of the royal drums or similar regalia – thereby linking their fortunes with those of the ruling house. Such office-holders were not drawn automatically from the same clans, a fact which suggests that in the process of establishing their authority the Babito had to turn to different groups at different times in order to win support.

Sir Tito Winyi, the royal historian of Bunyoro-Kitara, the name by which the empire came to be known, states that the first of the Babito rulers appointed chiefs in districts as far apart as Busongora and Bulega in the west, Bugungu and Chope, in the north, Bulemezi in the east and Nkore in the south, and that he and his immediate successors ruled over a peaceful land. However, his account of the life of the fourth Mukama, grandson of the founder of the dynasty, suggests that it was only in his reign, seventy years or more after the Babito came to Kitara, that a serious attempt was made to extend control beyond the limits of Buwekula, where the first capital was located, Kyaka and Mawogola.[8] This ruler, if the royal account is to be accepted, conducted a wide-ranging expedition to Kiziba on the south-western shore of Lake Victoria, then westward through Rwanda, before turning north to pass through Busongora and Bulega, presumably travelling to the west of the Ruwenzori Mountains, then across the Nile at Pakwach and southward through Acholi and Bugungu to Singo, where he built his capital and eventually died at Kiburara. His burial place is still to be found there, a thatched hut over a deep shaft in which the body of the Mukama was laid, the opening of the shaft being covered only by the hide of a bull pegged down by iron hoe heads.

That the passage of Mukama Winyi I through these regions was completely unopposed seems unlikely, but he is said to have appointed chiefs in Busongora and Bulega which probably means that this was the first time that the Babito were able to lay claim to the country so far to the west. In Bugungu and other regions to the north and south of the Victoria Nile Winyi was moving among people who had taken part in the Nilotic migration along with his own forefathers. Here he might well have been accepted, if not as absolute sovereign, at least as a powerful ruler whose friendship it was important to win and whose overlordship could be acknowledged without any embarrassment or loss of pride. It was probably during Winyi's stay at Kiburara, which is said to have covered many years, that regions such as Buyaga, Bugangaizi and Mwenge came under his control.

Olimi, Winyi's successor, is acknowledged to have been a warrior and was given the title 'conqueror of nations'. The saga of his travels contained in Sir Tito Winyi's account seems to border upon fantasy for it is claimed that he marched eastward as far as Nandi and Masai country and then, skirting the southern shores of Lake Victoria, returned through Sukumaland, Kiziba and Karagwe. Nevertheless, there can be no doubt that it was at this period of Bunyoro-Kitara's history that the extension of the empire towards the east was begun and that an attempt was also made to seize Nkore by force.

Although the detail of Sir Tito Winyi's account is not always accurate a general picture of the expansion of Babito control can be clearly discerned. The first step was to lay claim to the Bacwezi succession and to win control of the centre of the empire by enlisting the aid of the influential local clans. This took several decades and during that time the legend of the descent of the Babito from the Bacwezi was built up by every means available, including the conversion of what was originally a matrilineal link into a patrilineal relationship so that the Babito could claim to be the sons of the Bacwezi rather than the male descendants of an inferior race who had had the good fortune to marry Bacwezi wives.[9] Fortified by these means, later Bakama began to put out feelers to test the attitude of neighbouring districts to their pretensions. Soon the feelers could be backed by military strength so that even where the extension of the Mukama's authority was peacefully acknowledged this may well have been due to fear rather than to the recognition of his lawful right to rule.

The resistance shown by the inhabitants of some of the districts to the east differed in its origins from that put up by the Banyankore. Whatever the claims of the Bakama may have been it is fairly certain that Bacwezi domination had never extended eastward as far as the Nile where it flows from Lake Victoria to Lake Kyoga. The inhabitants of those regions, therefore, resented the Babito attempt to rule over the area. The opposition shown by the Banyankore, on the other hand, was due to the fact that their rulers also claimed descent from the Bacwezi and could not accept that the Babito had any prior claim to rule their country. So courageously did they resist that after a number of campaigns the Babito were eventually compelled to admit failure and had to content themselves with dominating a considerable territory to the north and east of Nkore. In time, too, the centre of the empire moved westward from Buwekula and the Bakama made their capitals mainly in Bugangaizi and Buyaga, where most of their burial places are to be found, though the bones of a few of them were laid to rest in more distant graves as a testimony either to the raids and wars of aggression in which they sometimes indulged to satisfy their pride and ambition or else to the difficulty of controlling the more remote districts of their empire.[10]

The Babito possessed no more adequate institutions for governing an extensive empire than did their predecessors, the Bacwezi, and in a land where communication was limited to journeys on foot, and where even then the going was not uniformly easy, it was difficult to create such institutions. Generally the Bakama resorted to the practice of selecting chiefs to administer different parts of their dominions on their behalf. Many of the persons thus appointed were themselves Babito, princes of the ruling dynasty, though royal birth was not a prerequisite of office. The Bakama, claiming sovereign powers by right of their descent from the Bacwezi, could appoint whomsoever they pleased. Members of the Babito clan were, however, a not unnatural choice for official appointments because they were well known to the Mukama and in the early stages at least, while they were strangers in the lands they administered, they were more likely to remain loyal to their sovereign because they leaned heavily upon his support. To maintain the supply of such chiefs the practice grew up of sending the sons of office holders, and particularly of members of the ruling family, to the district of Mwenge where many of the Mukama's herds were pastured and where the youths could learn the responsibilities and duties of office. In some districts, however, notably Buhweju and Buzimba, the existing ruling clans were retained but were deemed by the Bakama to be royal appointees although in their own eyes the relationship appeared to be one of suzerainty rather than of sovereignty.

Chieftainships were not automatically hereditary although in certain areas, in Kitagwenda for example, which was later to form part of the Kingdom of Toro, a dynasty of sub-chiefs developed at least as early as the eighteenth century. Nor did the Mukama restrict his appointments to men. Sometimes his daughters might become chiefs and exercise the same powers as those enjoyed by his sons. In such cases there could certainly be no question of establishing a hereditary dynasty of office-holders because the daughters of a Mukama were not permitted to marry.

Professor Beattie states that the authority exercised by the chiefs was territorial because the purpose of their appointment was to administer particular districts.[11] In those areas they were entitled to levy tribute from the inhabitants and they might also be required to exercise jurisdiction over any disputes which might arise. In return for the benefits of office they would be expected to make gifts to the Mukama from time to time and to levy an armed force to aid him in battle when called upon to do so. They might themselves appoint sub-chiefs by making grants of territorial administrative power within their own districts, but in theory at least such appointments were subject to the approval of the Mukama although he might send a representative to officiate at the installation rather than attending in person.

None of these appointments was intended to confer the right to exercise independent authority. The powers of the chiefs were deemed to be a manifestation of the sovereignty of the Mukama. Nevertheless, although this was the doctrine upheld by successive rulers the effectiveness of a Mukama's authority, as well as the area over which he might exercise it, clearly varied over the years, often reflecting the efficiency and personality of the Mukama himself as well as of his subordinates. In the early days, when the empire was still expanding and the vigour of the dynasty was as yet undiminished, there was little need to lay down any territorial boundaries, the hope being that the frontiers might be still further extended. In one area only was it thought useful to speak of a boundary and that was along the sternly contested frontier with the Kingdom of Buganda. There a swamp or river might be named as the dividing line between the spheres of authority of the Mukama of Bunyoro-Kitara and the Kabaka of Buganda, as Sir Tito Winyi's account at several points implies.

It would be difficult to define the northern limits of the empire because there were numerous chiefs in the region to the west of Lake Albert, and in Acholi and Lango too, who were pleased to acknowledge the ritual headship of the Mukama without necessarily accepting a relationship involving political subordination.[12] This latter kind of association played an important part in cementing the links between the Bakama and their chiefs even in the more closely integrated parts of the empire where office-holders were endowed with the authority of the Mukama by virtue of the ritual performed at their appointment when they became the personification of the Mukama's power. In some of the more distant parts, however, the Mukama's authority weighed lightly upon chiefs and people alike. It was not easy for the ruler, even with the aid of solemn ritual and with all the arguments of hereditary succession to support him, to exercise a rigid control throughout an empire of such wide extent. It was the practice of the Bakama to travel around their country to assert their authority as much as to fulfil their obligation to provide protection and justice for their people, but even this had its weaknesses for it left a gap at the centre. Although a ruler would leave a deputy with authority to act on his behalf this did not ensure either uniform or effective administration in his absence. There was, too, a further problem in that until the latter half of the nineteenth century the Bakama had no standing army or any other permanent force at his disposal to discipline his wayward subjects or to assist him in foreign wars. This resulted in a still greater emphasis being placed upon his supernatural powers and the sanction of hereditary right, but wherever possible more practical expedients were also employed. The Bakama insisted, for example, that each of the more senior office-holders should maintain a house at the capital and when the chief himself was not present he was required to provide a deputy to reside there in his stead. The chiefs of course were fully aware that it would be in their interests to keep in touch with the Mukama if they wished to remain in his favour. Frequent or prolonged absences from the capital might lead to the suspicion that they were plotting against him.

Nevertheless, chiefs did rebel from time to time, particularly, in later years, when a man happened to be a disappointed claimant to the succession to the throne. In such circumstances the Mukama would call upon his loyal subjects to rally to him in arms and would lead an expedition to put down the rising. One such rebellion took place in Koki in the eighteenth century, and although the rebel prince was defeated and killed his successor sought an alliance with the neighbouring kingdom of Buganda and from that time ceased to be politically subordinate to Bunyoro-Kitara. Even then the people of Koki found it difficult to shrug off all links with the past. Successive chiefs, and their subjects too, continued to visit Mubende, the site of Bunyoro-Kitara's first capital, to perform the rituals traditionally associated with events of importance to the clans.[13]

The duties of the Mukama were implicit in the various rituals associated with his accession. As the source of all power he was clearly responsible for the defence of the empire and in the absence of a standing army he had to rely upon levies, rather like Saxon fyrds, raised by his chiefs. Although demands for military aid must have caused considerable disruption to the lives of his subjects there does not appear to have been any serious objection to the fulfilment of this obligation except where chiefs were themselves hoping to make a bid for power. No doubt the people generally hoped for booty from the campaigns in which they were required to take part. It is difficult to estimate the extent to which their loyalty was aroused by their consciousness of belonging to a powerful empire. The pastoralist Bahima, for example, never held the Babito in very high regard, and the attitude of the rest of the population was probably determined more by the impact of an individual Mukama's rule upon their lives than upon any enthusiasm for the concept of empire. Indeed the Empire of Bunyoro-Kitara was so completely the creation of the Babito dynasty, and their claim to base the exercise of sovereign power upon their lawful descent from the Bacwezi was so important a factor in justifying their rule, that in theory at least no question of consent could arise.

Yet in the absence of any military force to support their authority popular approval was necessary and justice, mainly exercised by the imposition of fines, must be seen to be exercised fairly whether at the capital or while the Mukama was travelling through his dominions. In addition, although he was not himself a rainmaker he was regarded as head of the rainmakers whose duty it was to ensure that the needs of the people and of the cattle and the land were plentifully met. He was required, too, to encourage trade and might even take part in it himself.

In all his duties the Mukama had advisers who fell into different categories. Some were old men, constantly in close attendance upon him, who on account of their wisdom and experience were the most influential of his counsellors. He might also seek advice from any chief or official of his court and particularly from those men who had rendered him outstanding service or whose fathers had served his predecessors well and who as a reward were entitled to wear a crown of colobus monkey skin. At the same time he was not bound to accept the advice of any of these groups and a strong-minded or wilful Mukama might ignore them all and even act in an entirely contrary fashion in matters of the greatest moment. The sixth Mukama, Nyabongo I, grandson of Winyi I, undertook a campaign northward into Acholi in defiance of the warnings of his diviners. He appears to have been counselled on this occasion by his eldest son and it is indicative of the sovereign nature of the authority of a Mukama that he could afford to set aside even the most unfavourable of auguries.[14] Yet arbitrary or unpopular actions could bring their own retribution. Winyi II, for example, lost a great deal of support as a result of his harsh and high-handed behaviour. A Mukama, too, was expected to show largesse on all occasions although, if he were a strong ruler, this would not be difficult because he would receive gifts from many quarters, whether from those who had received benefits at his hand or from those who hoped to obtain benefits in the future.

A Mukama's wealth was mainly demonstrated by his ability to make generous gifts but the accumulation of wealth, except in cattle, was difficult because there was no currency and much of the produce of the country was of a perishable nature. This factor, too, assisted the Babito in maintaining a dominant position because the mainly agricultural population could not create economic reserves which might, over a long period, threaten the security of their ruler. Yet the Empire of Bunyoro-Kitara, if not wealthy, was certainly prosperous. Its prosperity rested upon a plentiful supply of foodstuffs, mainly grain and dairy produce, and a flourishing trade to help in the supply of other necessities and luxuries. A high proportion of the trade was carried on internally, between neighbours, anyone having any excess products or items such as goats, skins, pottery, tobacco, coffee beans or carpentry work, taking them for exchange at a local market, held at regular intervals, which also acted as a social centre. The largest of the markets was held near the Mukama's residence, and the exchange of news and conversation was as important as the barter of goods. There were therefore no professional traders or full-time store holders.

Not all the population was engaged in farming pursuits, for Bunyoro possessed two other important natural assets, iron and salt. Iron-smelting and the fashioning of hoes and spear-heads, techniques known to the Bantu long before the Nilotic incursions into western Uganda, developed into an important industry protected by rituals as exclusive as any medieval European guild system, and the Empire of Bunyoro-Kitara benefited from them accordingly. Workers in iron were greatly respected members of society, for their products, while improving the empire's agriculture and effectiveness in war, also compelled other states to seek friendship with Bunyoro-Kitara in order to acquire iron goods. There were, it would seem, no big centres of iron working, the industry being carried on by small groups of smiths in their own villages, and at its origin the trade in ironware took place in the local markets.[15] Because spears were part of the equipment of the adult male, for his personal defence and for protecting his herds against wild animals, and because there was no standing army, there was no need to build up an arsenal of weapons or for the Mukama to exercise total control over the industry. Nevertheless, he did accumulate a stock of spearheads and hoes, probably as gifts from tributaries, to be given in turn by him to others, and also to be used as inducements to assist the passage of emissaries through more distant lands.[16]

The lure of acquiring these items attracted would-be purchasers to Bunyoro-Kitara, although probably only to local markets where ironware was known to be available rather than to any main centres, and the buyers themselves may simply have bartered some of their purchases with their own neighbours, so making it unnecessary to have professional long-distance traders on any large scale. Nevertheless, some members of the empire may at times have acted as traders and transporters of ironware, for the extent of the trade was considerable, stretching along the shores of Lake Kyoga, where the recently arrived Langi and Iteso were introduced for the first time to the use of iron implements.[17] There was, too, a growing exchange trade with Buganda, which in its turn supplied plantains and bark cloth, the latter becoming the main form of material used in clothing the more important Banyoro.

An interesting feature of Bunyoro's trade in iron goods was the readiness with which spearheads were exported to states, particularly Buganda, with which Bunyoro was periodically at war. Even in the mid-nineteenth century, after Buganda had annexed Buddu with its own iron deposits and had become a serious threat to Bunyoro's security, the export of spearheads to Buganda continued freely.[18]

The trade in salt involved a number of different features. In the first place there were two areas where salt production was concentrated, at Kibero on Lake Albert, and at Lakes Katwe and Kasenyi in southern Busongora. Secondly, although salt was not immediately perishable it was more rapidly expended than hoes or spearheads and therefore more distant regions could not depend upon the slow filtration of salt from hand to hand or from one local market to another. Before the middle of the eighteenth century the trade had been largely an informal affair. Although people had come from far afield to bargain for salt, they had done so in small groups of eight or ten travellers who had made their way to the settlements upon the edge of the salt lakes bringing with them for exchange foodstuffs – millet, beans or honey – and iron implements of different kinds. A system of equivalents had developed to facilitate exchange and after spending a few days in barter and the nights in areas to which they returned on each visit, the traders started back for home. Those from distant regions carried smaller loads while those from near at hand humped larger bundles. When they reached their destinations they distributed the salt among their kinsmen and any that was left over was bartered to other villagers or to the inhabitants of neighbouring settlements.

The rapid expansion of the trade brought about a number of changes in its organization. In the first place the more frequent passage of traders through the surrounding country aroused a certain wariness and suspicion among the inhabitants which in turn encouraged the traders to travel in larger bands, armed with spears for self-protection. This made them appear more formidable to the people through whose country they passed and provoked further hostility. Some accommodation had to be reached and this was found in the ritual commonly called blood-brotherhood, but perhaps better described as the blood pact. By entering into a solemn contract of mutual good behaviour with the important people of each area through which they passed the traders were able to travel in safety. In return for safe passage a new category of authoritative and respected caravan leaders emerged who enforced discipline among the travellers.

Changes were simultaneously taking place at the salt lakes themselves. The Babito chief of Kisaka, the senior chief in Busongora, introduced the practice of appointing agents (*bahoza*) to ensure the more systematic collection of a tax in kind both from the salt producers and the traders who came to purchase salt. Characteristically, the agents were usually close kinsmen of the chief and a portion of his profit was of course sent as tribute to the ruler of Bunyoro. More important, however, was the arrival in the vicinity of Lakes Edward and George of two groups of people who had migrated by stages until one group, the Bagabo, settled on the islands in Lake George under the rule of a breakaway Babito dynasty, the Banyambaka. The other group, the Bakingo, occupied the two islands in Katwe Bay, in Lake Edward, and the shore beside Lake Katwe. They did not challenge the overlordship of the ruler of Kisaka, but they at once immersed themselves in the salt trade. They had brought with them fast, lightweight canoes and in them they began to transport salt to the further shores of Lakes Edward and George, shifting the main markets away from the salt lakes themselves and making the trade more accessible to travellers on foot from distant lands. The ruler of Kisaka was delighted by the enterprise and loyalty of these new subjects whose efforts resulted in a still more rapid growth in the trade and increased the income from the activities of the tax collectors. By the beginning of the nineteenth century, the Bagabo and Bakingo had ceased to grow their own food and were fully engaged in commerce and in mining salt. At the same time people were coming from still further afield, from Koki, from Buddu, from Bugangaizi, from Karagwe, and extending the range of trade goods they brought to include bark cloth and bananas from Buganda, coffee from Karagwe and the fine skins for which Bugangaizi was famous.[19]

Before the end of the eighteenth century all this pomp and prosperity was endangered. The dominant role claimed for so long by Bunyoro-Kitara was challenged by the growing power of Buganda. By the beginning of the nineteenth century the challenge was more persistent and more serious. There were, too, grave internal problems which no appeal to divine hereditary could avert. Kyebambe III had become Mukama by murdering his brother and in so doing had bequeathed to the succession a violent precedent which his sons and grandsons were not loath to inherit. It was this situation of decaying splendour which provided the opportunity for the emergence of the Kingdom of Toro. An empire over which the ruling dynasty had exercised only an uneven control even at its moment of greatest authority was cracking under the strain of internal and external pressures. The ruling dynasty retained office but its members, faced with the Buganda menace, preferred to pursue their individual interests instead of rallying to maintain the empire. The Bakama, who had frequently been compelled to connive at the near-independence of some of their chiefs, now saw their dominions still more blatantly carved up into local autonomies.

I · The Founding of the Kingdom

The Kingdom of Toro came into being because the grip of the Bakama upon the Empire of Bunyoro-Kitara was weakening and the appearance of unity which their rule had for generations imposed upon the fluctuating political scene in western Uganda was fading. But if the structure of empire was breaking up its spirit and customs survived, and Toro can only be understood as the offshoot of Bunyoro-Kitara. It was not initially conceived as a nation in the sense that its inhabitants believed themselves to possess a common heritage either of culture or experience. That such disparate peoples came together under one ruler is due to the fact that Toro was originally itself a miniature empire, aping the mores of its more extensive progenitor.[1] After the initial urge of the population to escape the clutches of Bunyoro had faded the only unifying force was the power of the ruler, and that power was exercised from the outset in the manner of the Bakama of Bunyoro.

Mukama Kyebambe III Nyamutukura took office in the latter part of the eighteenth century after overthrowing and killing his brother, Olimi IV. Wars of succession had been rare in earlier days, the ceremonial surrounding the death of a Mukama being designed to ensure secrecy until a successor acceptable to the leading chiefs was in an unassailable position.[2] In spite of the violent manner of his accession the earlier years of Nyamutukura's reign were nevertheless secure and he was even able to give assistance to Kakunguru, a prince of Buganda, in his struggle for power in his own country.[3] Later, however, the Mukama's reign became one of almost continuous strife. Bikunya states that this was due in part to the fact that Nyamutukura performed the *njeru* ceremony after which a

Mukama was supposed to hand over effective government of the country to the *mugema* (a senior chief) and two or three other senior chiefs and to forswear involvement in war.[4] Outlying districts were thus encouraged to rebel against his rule and his sons joined in the struggle. Nyakatura agrees[5] that Nyamutukura performed the *njeru* ceremony and this was confirmed by the then *mugema* in 1951 in conversation with the author. Both these two informants, however, attributed the disloyalty of the princes primarily to Nyamutukura's longevity which prevented them from assuming the power which many of them coveted.

The first to strike was Karasuma who sought the assistance of Kabaka Kamanya of Buganda in an attempt to overthrow his father. Accounts of his reception by the Kabaka differ but he was certainly unsuccessful in his bid for power, whether he was killed by the Kabaka at the request of Nyamutukura as some authorities claim[6] or by the Mukama himself, as a later Mukama, Duhaga IV, maintained. Duhaga also said that behind this and other later plots was the scheming of Kacope, another son of the Mukama, who hoped to seize power himself and planned to do it by destroying all his brothers.[7] Kacope, however, subsequently withdrew to his own district of Chope in the northern part of the empire to consolidate his rule there, and although he ceased to be a claimant for the throne his district remained a source of endless trouble to later Bakama.

The next to attempt a break with the Mukama was Kaboyo, who was by all accounts Nyamutukura's favourite, though he was extremely unpopular with many of the chiefs. Even his grandson, Kasagama, who admired him, said that he indulged in practical jokes which angered his brothers and he was not above scheming to take them at a disadvantage.[8] Kaboyo was a tall young man with a powerful frame; he was vigorous and extrovert in his behaviour but he did not lack cunning when it was needed. The exercise of authority was a habit with him as it was with the other Babito princes, and in accordance with custom his father had made him a chief on the borders of

Mwenge and Burahya counties. He had also requested him to collect tribute in the district to the south, among the foothills of the Ruwenzoris and in the area to the east of the mountains. This was the country inhabited by Bakonjo and Batoro agriculturalists, many of whom had taken refuge in the area to get away from their own clans and to escape from the authority of the Mukama. The region had been administered earlier by a commoner acting on behalf of the Mukama and more recently by two of Nyamutukura's daughters. But the people accepted authority with the greatest reluctance, and when Kaboyo arrived in their midst and befriended some of them they hatched a plot to support the young prince in an attempt to break with the Mukama and make the district independent.[9]

It is not clear where the idea of a rebellion originated though it is possible that the Batoro and Bakonjo sensed Kaboyo's restlessness and so took the initiative in proposing it to him. What they hoped to gain by the venture is uncertain. It seems unlikely that they aimed to replace a resented but remote authority by a more local and potentially more oppressive ruler. Perhaps they hoped that a prince of their own would protect them against external predators and limit the number of those entitled to make demands upon them. Certainly they were no lovers of monarchy and if they sought to improve their lot by assisting Kaboyo their hopes proved ill-founded.

The young prince did not raise the standard of rebellion immediately. First he returned to the capital to enlist the help of a number of his friends who willingly offered to participate in the enterprise in the hope of gaining power and booty. To get these men away required careful planning and Kaboyo was forced to resort to a variety of subterfuges before he was finally able to deceive his father and make good his escape. As soon as he was safely back on the borders of Toro, however, he declared war. It was not his intention to supplant Nyamutukura. He simply wanted to carve out a kingdom for himself from within the empire.

The Mukama could not afford to see his authority flouted even by his favourite son, and although he was himself unable to go to war because he had taken part in the *njeru* ceremony, he sent an army to put down the rising. There was heavy fighting, but eventually the Mukama's forces were defeated. To add to his discomfiture the Baganda, taking advantage of this setback and seeking revenge for the assistance given by Nyamutukura to Kakunguru, invaded the country from the east and drove the Banyoro armies across the Kafu River. The ageing Mukama took temporary refuge on an island in Lake Albert and from there attempted to bring about a reconciliation with Kaboyo. Mrs Fisher's account[10] attributes this move to the intervention of another son, Mugenyi, chief of Mwenge, who did not aspire to succeed his father and who had remained loyal to him throughout his many tribulations. Mugenyi, Mrs Fisher states, urged Nyamutukura to make common cause with Kaboyo against the Baganda, setting aside old differences. Kasagama, however, writing from the Toro standpoint, suggests that the Mukama was mainly influenced by his long-standing affection for his son and it was this feeling which, on reflection, led him to set aside his resentment and seek Kaboyo's friendship. As an earnest of his new mood the Mukama sent his son a drum named Butwarana, together with the message *Naiwe obege okitiyo oku*. This phrase can be translated 'Very well, stay where you are', but its construction implies kindness as well as censure, and the gift of the drum suggests that the Mukama was prepared to accept his son's overlordship of Toro.

In spite of Mrs Fisher's claim that part of the agreement between the Mukama and Kaboyo envisaged south Toro becoming independent of Bunyoro with Kaboyo exercising the right to nominate his own successor,[11] it seems unlikely that Nyamutukura intended to allow the establishment of a permanently independent state in Toro. In all probability he looked upon his son's action as a typically impetuous claim to authority about which he could not at the moment take any steps. It would not, however, have any serious long-term implications since Kaboyo was likely to succeed him as Mukama and Toro would then be peacefully reunited with the empire.

Kaboyo's own view of his position was probably very different, but it is significant that his subjects never gave him the royal greeting of '*Okali*'[12] (a word of Nilotic origin). For them, and even more for the inhabitants of the heartland of the empire, his power was never sovereign. Karubanga, a true Munyoro, wrote, 'Of all these princes [sons of Nyamutukura] only Mugenyi became king',[13] while Sir Tito Winyi also described Kaboyo as only a prince. Kaboyo nevertheless acted in all respects as an independent ruler. Having made peace with his father with whom he remained on good terms for the rest of the latter's life, sending him gifts of cattle from time to time and requiring his sub-chiefs to show respect to the old Mukama, he proceeded to consolidate his position in his new kingdom.

The immediate outcome of the royal reconciliation was that the Baganda were driven back beyond the Kafu River but were able to hold on to the territory as far west as Wesigire and Kabyoma, near Mubende, the first capital of the Empire of Bunyoro-Kitara.[14] Mugenyi, the faithful son, went to live with Nyamutukura to support him in his old age. Kaboyo, meanwhile, established his first capital at Buhesi, some eight miles, as the crow flies, south-west of the present town of Fort Portal. The Bakonjo who had assisted Kaboyo in his war with the Mukama were apprehensive about their relations with the young ruler. In an attempt to win their confidence he therefore summoned a number of them to drink beer with him. Not without misgivings they accepted his invitation, and they were partially reassured when Kaboyo asked them to drink from the same pot from which he himself was drinking. They warily watched, however, to see his Adam's apple move so that they knew he was swallowing the beer, before they themselves were prepared to drink. But Kaboyo was too clever for them. He had no intention of drinking with the Bakonjo, whom he regarded as his subjects and inferior to him in every way. What they took to be a drinking straw in his hand was a stick, and he only made a pretence of swallowing the beer. It was enough to reassure the Bakonjo, however. They left to circulate among the people the news that Kaboyo was to be trusted, that he was no remote chief but was eminently approachable, and that he thought well of those among whom he had come to live.

That the Bakonjo had misjudged their man became obvious in time, but not immediately. Over several years Kaboyo acquired a reputation for taking an energetic interest in developing the agricultural resources of Toro. Moving around the countryside in his splendid robes of rich red bark cloth, he kept a watchful eye for signs of sloth among his subjects, never hesitating to beat any man or woman whom he saw idling in the fields. But his censure was counterbalanced by an impulsive generosity. He readily rewarded good work with gifts – butter in a traditional container for the woman, perhaps, or a young bull for a man. So constantly was he to be found mixing with his people that he was given the name *Munywani* (friend).

His association with Toro proved wholly satisfying to Kaboyo who enjoyed the experience of total responsibility which his new office offered, and there was scope, too, for further expansion to the south and east. Even when his father died some five years after the breakaway of Toro, therefore, Kaboyo did not regard himself as a claimant to the succession. In spite of his respect for Nyamutukura he rejected his brother Mugenyi's invitation to take part in the ceremonial mourning rites. Mugenyi, who was still chief of Mwenge, then approached his brothers in turn urging them to accept the succession. Kacope, who according to Mrs Fisher had at one time wanted to become Mukama, no longer had any relish for the position: with Kaboyo firmly entrenched in Toro, Mugenyi in Mwenge and the Baganda a constant threat to the Empire, the precarious role of ruler of Bunyoro-Kitara had no attraction for the chief of the northern provinces. Kaboyo similarly rejected the honour, claiming that he was content with what he had and clearly preferring the experience of real power to the doubtful pleasures of becoming overlord of a crumbling empire, divided within itself and harassed from without. Reluctantly Mugenyi became Mukama, adopting the name of Nyabongo II.

A peace-loving man, Mugenyi was fortunate that his mother was the twin sister of the mother of Kabaka Suna of Buganda, so that danger from that quarter was temporarily averted. His brothers, however, while indifferent to the succession, caused him some harassment in the north,[15] while Kasagama mentions briefly that Kaboyo sent an army against Mugenyi's son, Katamera, who had succeeded his father as chief of Mwenge, and in the ensuing battle Katamera was defeated. This was only one of Kaboyo's acts of aggression when he had become ruler of Toro. The chronological sequence of events in his career is not certain, but it is possible to obtain a reasonably clear impression of his aims and of how he set about achieving them. Toro itself, in spite of its agricultural potential, covered only a small area at this stage of his career. It was probably no more than 500 square miles in extent, comprising the present counties of Bunyangabo, Burahya and the western extremities of Mwenge and Kibale. To a man of Kaboyo's energy this could scarcely have seemed an adequate inheritance.

His first venture in extending his authority is not easily explained. Kasagama mentions it only briefly. He states that 'Kaboyo had already acquired Bugereke, now called Congo, in the course of another war.' The region referred to is probably the northern end of the Ruwenzori Mountains, including part of the forests of Bwamba and possibly stretching as far as the Semliki River valley. The attractions of this area are not immediately obvious. Bwamba had no economic potential and although the well-watered plains of the Semliki valley may have appealed to Kaboyo's eye for good grazing ground, to get there meant descending the escarpment which acted as a useful defensive bulwark on Toro's northern frontier.

More understandable was the later campaign into Busongora, which at the time extended as far north as the Mubuku River, thus covering a considerably larger area than does the modern county of the same name. The salt deposits of Lake Katwe not only promised to fulfil an important need of the people of Toro but, if brought under Kaboyo's control, would be both a significant source of wealth and an addition to his bargaining power in dealing with his neighbours. In addition, the plains of Busongora were well stocked with cattle. Kaboyo had no more personal claim to this area than to Bugereke, but at one time or another both areas had been deemed to form part of the Empire of Bunyoro-Kitara. According to Kasagama, Nyamutukura had tried to reincorporate Busongora within the Empire by force of arms but had failed, and the imperial commander had been killed in battle. The new Mukama, Mugenyi, lacked the power and the inclination to reassert imperial authority in this remote area and in any case was compelled to devote his main military effort to campaigning against the rebellious factions in Chope. The manner in which Busongora had seceded from the empire had, however, left it at risk if a more powerful conqueror should seek to annex it. Kaboyo was such a man.

The conquest of Busongora was not an easy undertaking, nor does the country appear to have been annexed as the result of one single battle. The course of the campaign and the gradual extension of Kaboyo's authority can be traced from the locations in which the invaders established temporary headquarters. The first of these was on the spit of land between the rivers Kitajuka and Mubuku, a position of considerable tactical strength and one from which an attack might be launched with comparative ease. Here, however, Kaboyo had to abandon his campaign when it had scarcely begun. News reached him that two of his sons whom he had appointed as chiefs, one in a more northerly part of Toro and the other on the very borders of Busongora itself, had rebelled. He was faced with a problem similar to that with which he had presented his own father.

Moreover, because he had renounced all right to the imperial succession his only claim to rule in Toro was based upon his military strength. Although his sons, in taking advantage of the preoccupation of their overlord in other parts of the country, were behaving as Bunyoro princes had done in outlying parts of the empire for generations, they were at the same time asserting a claim to test their strength against that of another man who ruled purely by conquest.

On this occasion the attempt to overthrow the power of Kaboyo failed completely. The challengers mustered their forces at Rusekere, about eight miles north-east of Fort Portal. Kaboyo marched against them at the head of only a small army because he had to leave a strong holding force on the frontiers of Busongora to prevent a counter-attack from that quarter. He made his camp at Bwanika, just to the north-west of Fort Portal, and from this base he advanced to join battle. The two armies met at Kikongo and Kaboyo was victorious. His sons, Kamara and Musaga, were captured and brought before their father who summarily ordered their execution. No considerations of paternal affection were permitted to interfere with the punishment of men who were willing to rebel at such a critical moment for the future of the kingdom. Even Kaboyo's own father, who had loved him dearly, had tried, if unsuccessfully, to chastise him when he himself had cast adrift, and neither of the two rebellious sons held the place in Kaboyo's heart which he himself had occupied in the heart of Nyamutukura.

Having dealt with the insurrection Kaboyo turned again southward and resumed his campaign against Busongora. Stage by stage he advanced his control over the country, partly by persuasion, partly by military conquest. Kasagama lists the villages which became Kaboyo's temporary headquarters, sometimes for as little as two months, more often for a year or more. Kanyampara, for example, standing astride the track which skirts the southern foothills of the Ruwenzoris, beside the river which bears the same name, was Kaboyo's base for a year while he marshalled his strength to seize the salt lakes, twelve miles further south and one of the main targets of his campaign.

Kaboyo's experience with his rebellious sons in the north did not discourage him from following the long-standing Bunyoro practice of appointing other sons and grandsons as chiefs, responsible for parts of the conquered territory, in place of those deposed for resisting his advance. In days of poor communications and vast distances a ruler had little alternative but to rely upon the loyalty of others, but it was not until the reign of Kabarega in Bunyoro-Kitara that a Mukama was able to shrug off dynastic claims and recognize that sons and grandsons were less reliable subordinates than men whose positions depended not on birth but upon the benevolence of their overlord. Kaboyo himself, and still more his successors, were to suffer grievously from family disloyalty, but in the meantime the riches of the salt lakes were a temporary balm to the wounds of the campaigners.

Kaboyo's inheritance in Busongora was a valuable one and he made sure that appropriate tribute was paid to him and that the trade in salt remained under his close control. Very soon, too, a new dimension was added to this commerce. Baziba and Bahaya traders from the south-east, journeying to Lake Edward and Lake George in search of salt and bringing with them cotton goods and cowrie shells from the east coast, took back news of the vast herds of elephant which roamed in Bunyaruguru, Igara, Kitagwenda, Rujumbura and in parts of Toro. Arab and Swahili traders, who in the second quarter of the nineteenth century were beginning to penetrate into the heart of the African continent from their bases in Zanzibar and Bagamoyo, received the news with avidity. Ivory, which was of no interest to the inhabitants of the lake regions who hunted elephants only for food, and that on no very extensive scale, had a great attraction for the men of the coast because it fetched a good price in the world market.

The Baziba and Bahaya traders were, therefore, responsible for opening up a new trade on the borders of Kaboyo's kingdom. At first they purchased the tusks from African hunters and themselves carried their booty to markets further south where they exchanged the ivory for coast goods. But soon the voracious demand for this new source of wealth lured the Swahili traders into the ivory-producing regions where they were later followed by the Arabs. Initially, arrangements to regulate the new trade developed on an informal basis. A man who killed an elephant would give one tusk to his chief and sell the other to the traders, but there were many ways in which it was possible to evade the payment of dues to the chiefs. The latter, seeing the trade expanding and the Swahili themselves hunting and killing elephants, determined to impose the sort of controls which would ensure that they were paid their rightful tribute and that foreigners should not range unchecked through their territories. A further factor made official intervention a matter of urgency; the coastal traders brought not only cotton goods and cowrie shells but also firearms and gunpowder. The rulers of the states of western Uganda could not permit the indiscriminate sale of such potent weapons to their subjects. The trade must be in their hands alone. For these important reasons royal markets were opened where the ivory could be exchanged under the eye of the rulers' agents.

Toro was probably less directly affected by this new development than were some of her immediate neighbours. Busongora itself had few elephants and the salt trade remained as important as ever because the demand for salt remained unchanged. There were, it is true, elephants further north in Bunyangabo and Burahya and although few of the Swahili traders visited Busongora, a few travelled through Kitagwenda to do business in Toro itself. The kingdom, however, remained on the fringes of the new commercial developments and in so doing escaped almost completely the other more disastrous element of the coastal trade, the capture of slaves.

The relative isolation from the new forces which were disturbing the neighbouring countryside may have had its benefits for Toro at the time when that country was in need of a period of peace and orderly administration if it were to become a kingdom in any united sense. But Kaboyo cannot have been unaware of the potential danger to his position arising from the trade in firearms. Mukama Kamrasi of Bunyoro, who had taken office after supplanting and killing his brother, Olimi V, in about 1852, and whose country was rich in ivory, had every need of all available weapons to stave off the threats which came from both within and without the Empire, and so he encouraged the trade with the men from the coast. A regular trade route developed through Kitagwenda and Mwenge to Kamrasi's capital near Masindi, a route which became increasingly important to the Arab and Swahili traders when their trade with Buganda was shut off for a time in the mid-1850s while the new Kabaka, Mutesa, was establishing himself on the throne in the face of vigorous rivalry from his brothers.

It was probably during the period when ivory supplies were curtailed by the closing of Buganda's frontiers that east coast traders made their way to the port of Magungo on the Victoria Nile near the northern tip of Lake Albert and in the northernmost part of Kamrasi's empire. Sir Samuel Baker, for example, in his account of his discovery of Lake Albert, writes that he met inhabitants of the southern Sudan who claimed to have seen pale-skinned men riding donkeys in Magungo, men who had come by canoe from the south bringing with them cowrie shells with which to trade. Their visits had, however, died away in the early 1860s, no doubt when the road to Buganda had again been opened.[16] While it is possible that the traders had approached the southern shores of Lake Albert by an overland route through Mwenge or Buyaga it seems unlikely that, having reached either of those areas, they should not then have pursued a more natural path to Kamrasi's capital. More probably they followed the Semliki River from Lake Edward, round the western slopes of the Ruwenzori Mountains, and there are a number of suggestions that this route, mainly by water and closely paralleling the land route followed by Henry Morton Stanley in company with Emin Pasha in 1889, was not unknown.[17]

Encircled by the new forces which heralded a revolution in the affairs of the Lake Region, Kaboyo remained secure from external threats mainly because his potential rivals were themselves too deeply engaged by more immediate problems. The usurper, Mukama Kamrasi, was himself threatened by other rival princes from the northern parts of his empire. Although many of these rebels were killed in battle, two, Ruyonga and Mpuhuka, escaped and were able to harass if not seriously to challenge the Mukama from island bases in the Victoria Nile for the remainder of his reign. In addition, Bunyoro and Buganda had again begun to snarl at each other like angry dogs when the accession of Mukaabya (Mutesa) in 1857 put an end to the truce between the two countries which had marked Suna's reign. Mukaabya launched a series of raids against Busoga to the east and Bunyoro to the west. In the course of one of these latter attacks Baganda armies reached the shores of Lake Albert, forcing Kamrasi to take refuge on an island in the River Nile.[18]

Both Bunyoro and Buganda were wary of the influence which foreign traders might wield. Kamrasi in particular was conscious of a new menace from the activities of ivory traders and slave hunters from Khartoum. These raiders had begun to penetrate into Acholi, north of the Victoria Nile, in the early 1860s and the news of their depredations and ruthlessness, as well as the devastating power of their firearms, was not long in reaching Kamrasi's capital. Meanwhile the raiders themselves drew rapidly closer to Bunyoro, lured by the elephant herds which roamed there. They crossed the Nile in 1863 and at once Kamrasi was caught up in a new struggle to protect his position. By the time the traders from Zanzibar reached the country to the north of Lake Victoria they were so far from their bases that they had to behave with circumspection when they encountered powerful African rulers. The Khartoumers, however, had no such scruples. Having hitherto met no serious opposition they were full of confidence in their ability to overawe any African ruler who might stand in their path or, failing that, to overcome any resistance he might try to muster. In Kamrasi's case they had the added advantage of discovering a ready-made force for subversion in Ruyonga and the other rivals of the Mukama whom they met on their island strongholds in the Nile before they came upon Kamrasi himself.[19]

Only a year earlier both Buganda and Bunyoro had encountered a further external phenomenon in the shape of two European explorers, John Speke and James Grant, who had travelled to Buganda from the East African coast, rounding the western shores of Lake Victoria. From Buganda they had moved on to Bunyoro before disappearing northward, down the Nile. Although these men had seemed to possess phenomenal powers as well as a variety of objects, including guns, of a far better quality than those brought by the Zanzibari traders, they had not in themselves offered any overt threat to the position of either Mutesa or Kamrasi. They were obviously dependent upon their African hosts for everyday necessities, particularly for food, and they were not accompanied by any numerous following. What their visit might portend, who might come in their footsteps, were, however, matters of concern to Kamrasi in particular.

In February 1864 there arrived from the north another white man, Samuel Baker, accompanied by his wife and claiming friendship with the earlier travellers. The Bakers did not come alone. With them were some of the dreaded Khartoumers. The choice of travelling companions was not one which Baker would have made if there had been any alternative, but the power now exercised by the slavers over the country between Khartoum and Bunyoro was so great that he could have made no progress without their cooperation. Nor was Baker the sort of man to rely upon soft words and a gentle demeanour to ingratiate himself with the Africans he met. Unfortunately for his good relations with the people through whose country he travelled Baker, like many other enterprising Victorians who found their way to distant lands, believed that a bold, even an aggressive manner, was the most effective way to illustrate the unquestionable superiority of Englishmen over all foreigners, and particularly over ill-clad, apparently poverty-stricken savages such as he had come across in Africa. Baker was far from being a natural bully. He simply believed that any sign of weakness on his part would encourage Africans to take advantage of him.

It was not surprising, in view of his bombast and of the company in which he came, that Baker was not received by Kamrasi himself, who feared treachery, but by a prince masquerading as the Mukama.[20] Nor was the situation improved when Baker discovered the subterfuge weeks later and automatically attributed it to Kamrasi's innate deceitfulness. Although he intervened later in the year to protect the Mukama from an attack by a party of Khartoumers,[21] Baker's departure was greeted with relief, mingled with apprehension lest he and the Khartoumers should return with greater force and with even more destructive effect.

Little is known of Kaboyo's relations with his neighbours while these events, full of omens for the future, were taking place in the neighbouring kingdoms. It is said that at some time towards the end of his reign he sent his son, Kato, to Nkore, presumably on a mission of friendship and possibly to avoid military intervention from that quarter. For, although the Kingdom of Nkore upon which the colonial kingdom of Ankole was later to be built was still of only limited extent, the military reputation of Mutambuka, the *Mugabe* (ruler), was growing rapidly. Kato made friends with Mutambuka's son and presumed successor, Rukongyi, who, however, on his father's death was murdered by a supporter of his brother, Mukwenda, a rival claimant to the succession. Kaboyo's initiative was nevertheless to produce unforeseen results during the reign of another of his sons, Nyaika Kasunga.

There is no clear indication of the length of Kaboyo's reign. Kasagama says that he lived to the age of seventy or eighty, but the date of his rebellion against his father can be fixed only very tentatively at about 1830 and there is no evidence to suggest Kaboyo's age at that time, so the question is little advanced by speculation in this quarter. Nor is the statement that his half-brother, Mugenyi, was reluctant to succeed his father as Mukama of Bunyoro because he himself was well-advanced in years at the time of Nyamutukura's death,[22] a great help because the age range of the sons of a Mukama as long-lived as Nyamutukura was likely to have been considerable. Several things suggest that Kaboyo reigned until the late 1860s, though none is conclusive. Kasagama's account of the struggle for the succession after Kaboyo's death, for example, indicates a short but vigorous sequence of events prior to a raid by Buganda which Kaggwa says took place in 1871,[23] a date confirmed by Kasagama in his *Memoir*. Kaggwa's dating is open to some question, however, and there is a possibility that Kasagama may have telescoped his narrative as did also Sir Tito Winyi and Kaggwa himself on occasion. Against this is the fact that Nyaika was Kasagama's father so that although the latter was only a very young child at the time when the events took place which he later described, it is probable that he had an accurate knowledge of their sequence.

An interesting aspect of Kasagama's record of Kaboyo's reign is that he makes only a brief reference to the character of his grandfather's administration, virtually the whole account being taken up with a description of military campaigns for the extension or maintenance of Kaboyo's authority. While the reign may indeed have been filled to some extent with warfare there must have been long periods of peace, but Kasagama's *Memoir* resembles most other accounts of the reigns of the rulers of the kingdoms of western Uganda in being concerned primarily with recording the extent rather than the nature of the ruler's authority. Even in its extent, however, Kaboyo's power could not have been great. At his most effective he may have controlled the counties of Bunyangabo, Burahya, Busongora and the western portions of Mwenge and Kibale. This was virtually the area assumed by Lugard in 1890 to have belonged to the former kingdom with, however, the surprising addition of Kitagwenda to which Kaboyo never laid claim.

The nature of Kaboyo's government in many ways followed the pattern of Bunyoro monarchy. He quickly established himself as the source of all authority, and along with that authority went the responsibility for maintaining and administering justice and of defending his people against external aggression. He shared his sovereignty with no one, although he was free to take advice where he wished. He asserted, too, his right to levy such tribute as he deemed appropriate, and the only people in any position to question his claims were the Banyoro notables who had shared with him in his rebellion and who could see his authority in its true light. They, however, had no occasion to raise difficulties, for their prosperity was so closely linked up with his own. To them he gave gifts of land and, as the Bakama had done for generations past, he granted to those of his associates who had accompanied him from the imperial capital and who had served him well in his bid for independence the right to wear the *kondo*, the crown of colobus monkey skin. For the closer administration of the country he appointed his sons as chiefs of districts in accordance with Bunyoro practice.

The people who did not profit from Kaboyo's largesse were the Batoro and Bakonjo who, having rallied to his aid at the time of the rebellion, now for the greater part found themselves subject to Banyoro chiefs who levied tribute from them while bringing them no greater security than they had formally been able to enjoy through their own unaided efforts. They, however, were in no position to challenge Kaboyo's power. While, therefore, some continued loyal to their new rulers others remained where they were, cherishing their resentment until, a century later, they could seize the opportunity to show their displeasure. Yet others, particularly the Bakonjo, disillusioned by Kaboyo's apparent ingratitude, adopted the customary method of demonstrating their distrust by moving away from his sphere of influence to pursue their independence once again among the foothills of the Ruwenzoris. There they preserved their feelings of betrayal until they were able to demonstrate to a wider audience their rejection of the new ruling dynasty in Toro. For their part, Kaboyo and his chiefs developed a contempt for the Bakonjo and Batoro upon whose good faith they had traded, dismissing them as mere agriculturists, uncivilized people incapable of appreciating strong government.

There is little evidence, save of a retrospective character, regarding the social life of Toro during this period. The change of masters probably had little effect upon the day-to-day activities of the people, and the natural life cycle of the farmers doubtless continued with occasional interruptions when warfare raged across the country and when men were called upon to defend their homes or to flee with their families and possessions to the security of the mountains when fortune favoured their enemies. In time of peace the millet or the sweet potatoes would be planted and harvested, the herdsmen would tend their cattle, sheep and goats, and domestic or communal tasks would be carried out as they had always been. Thatched huts destroyed by storms would be rebuilt, and agricultural land ravaged by elephants would be restored to order when the elephants themselves had been driven off or hunted and killed so that all could eat the meat. Births were celebrated and deaths lamented with the ceremony inherited from Banyoro or even more remote ancestors. Festivities would mark the passing seasons and drumming, dancing and beer drinking would satisfy the needs of both joy and sorrow.

There is, it is true, no record of all this. One can only assume that things were as they had always been after allowance has been made for manners and customs which could only have arisen as a result of alien intervention. The songs that were sung, telling of significant events in the past, would vary depending upon the earlier origins of those who sang them. Yet, with modifications to adjust to more recent developments, they were doubtless the same as those sung by their forefathers and now sung by their descendants. Changes there undoubtedly were, for society in Toro may have been traditional but it was not static. The education of children might be designed less to introduce them to philosophical enquiry than to fit them for participation in the age-old ways of their family, but that did not mean that the people of the new kingdom were incapable of adjusting their ways and adapting themselves to new situations when they arose. Had they been unable to do so they could never have survived.

One thing is clear, the life Kaboyo's people led did not greatly encourage the development of arts or crafts. Some huts, particularly those of important people, had gaily decorated walls, but pictorial art was not otherwise greatly in evidence. Fine basket work was a traditional craft of Bunyoro and continued to find a place in Toro too. In general, however, arts and crafts were the product of the economic life of the country rather than something developed for their own sake or imposed by alien masters. The tools many used were those best suited to their trade. Small refinements there might be, but fundamental changes there were none unless overwhelming circumstances made necessary the adoption of an entirely new way of life as, for example, when an outbreak of rinderpest might force pastoralists, willy-nilly, to resort to agriculture to maintain themselves.

If, however, the people of Toro seemed safe from catastrophe at the close of Kaboyo's reign theirs was a precarious security. Soon the kingdom was to be torn by internal strife, shattered by external conquest and only revived by the unexpected intervention of a *deus ex machina* in the shape of a British army captain, seeking in Victorian fashion to heal a broken heart and satisfy his pride by forcing astonished Africans to accept his leadership and the benefits of association with a remote and indifferent British Government.

II · The Kingdom Destroyed

Kaboyo's reign had been taken up in sporadic campaigning to extend and then to maintain his newly acquired kingdom; his death plunged the country into an even greater turmoil. The monarchy had provided the only element of unity that Toro possessed and the binding force of Kaboyo's overlordship had been fragile at all times. The custom of putting sons and other relations in charge of districts created too many centres of potential rivalry to the overall authority of the ruler. This weakness was immediately demonstrated when the succession was challenged within months of Kaboyo's death. His immediate successor was his son, Kazana, but the latter had scarcely assumed office when another son, Nyaika Kasunga, assembled a faction to support his claim to power. In spite of Nyaika's popularity Kazana was able to stave off the first attack and to pursue his brother towards Mwenge. Nyaika then feigned sickness and his supporters brought the news to Kazana, suggesting that his rival no longer constituted any threat to his authority and could safely be allowed to return to Toro. By this subterfuge Nyaika's well-wishers were able to make good their earlier setback and their leader's homecoming was turned into a triumph.

It was now Kazana's turn to flee and, heading southward, he sought refuge in the kingdom of Nkore where he asked for military support. Karugire makes no mention of this appeal and the account of Kazana's flight is based upon Kasagama's *Memoir*. But there seems no good reason to reject the view that Mutambuka, the Mugabe of Nkore, was willing enough to respond, and Karugire's references to two raids carried out by Mutambuka against Busongora[1] would fit into the pattern of events described by Kasagama. Endowed with an aggressive personality the Mugabe was also a man of considerable military talent. Even in the days of his grandfather, Mugabe Rwebishengye, he had established a reputation for generalship and he had been largely responsible for bringing his father, Gasyonga, to the throne despite a strong challenge from the latter's brother, Kayunga.

During Gasyonga's reign Mutambuka was the leading military figure in Nkore, but it was only when he himself became Mugabe that his warlike spirit found complete fulfilment. He was fortunate to have at his disposal the elements of a useful military force. With the decline of Bunyoro, Nkore had been for some time relatively free from any threat from the north. More recently new dangers had arisen, particularly in the east where Kabaka Suna of Buganda had taken advantage of his country's growing strength to launch military campaigns against his neighbours. In the time of Gasyonga Nkore was raided on three occasions by the Baganda who, however, appeared to be content with making off with women and cattle and made no pretence of occupying territory. In response to these new dangers both Rwebishengye and Gasyonga created a number of military units, and Mutambuka, who inherited the system, developed it further by associating military leadership with the responsibilities of territorial administration.[2]

This measure changed the whole character of Nkore government which hitherto had consisted mainly in the administration of justice by the monarch. Faced now with an entirely new situation the Banyankore were fortunately in a position to meet the challenge. Indeed, Mutambuka went further, conducting successful campaigns in the direction of Lake George against Buhweju, which formerly had been able to defy even the might of Bunyoro in its heyday, thanks to a combination of courage and the skilful use of the natural advantages offered by its mountainous terrain. From Mutambuka's time Buhweju paid tribute to Nkore while the minor states to the north-east,

Buzimba and Kitagwenda, which until now had been tributaries of Bunyoro, switched their allegiance to Nkore as an insurance against invasion from that quarter.[3]

To a man of Mutambuka's character and ability the opportunity to intervene in the affairs of a neighbouring state was a temptation not to be ignored. Although he probably had no intention of acquiring territory for himself it was clearly to his advantage to have a neighbour who was indebted to him for his throne yet who, from the very nature of his accession, was unlikely to constitute a threat to Nkore. In any case, there was always a prospect of acquiring cattle. The Mugabe therefore placed a military force at Kazana's disposal and, thus reinforced, the latter returned to Toro to pursue his claim to the throne. Mutambuka's military success against Buhweju had given the armies of Nkore easy access to the Kazinga Channel and it is probable that the invading force crossed first into Busongora, a region where restless spirits abounded and support for a rebellion was readily forthcoming. Kazana's hopes of success were, however, quickly dispelled. Nyaika's supporters were too numerous and when the invaders came up against his army they were heavily defeated. Kazana retreated northward and tried to make a stand at the strategic frontier post of Rusekere where Kaboyo had defeated the army of Nyamutukura. At this late stage Kato, another brother of the rival contenders, who had halted at Ibanda on the northern borders of Busongora while on his way to help Kazana, now tried to come to the latter's aid, but Nyaika interposed his army between the two. Simultaneously he sent to Kamuhanda, Mukama Mugenyi's son who was chief of Mwenge, offering a bribe if he would kill Kazana. Kamuhanda responded willingly by sending an expedition to Rusekere, and Nyaika's rival was eliminated.

Even now Nyaika's position was far from secure. The main threat still came from Busongora where several of his brothers and nephews held chieftainships, and where even Kaboyo had been able to exercise only minimal authority towards the end of his reign. These princes lived in some state. Stanley, passing through Busongora in 1889 when the country had been subjected to military invasion, commented upon the excellence of the chiefs' huts, one of which was twenty feet in height and about twenty-five feet in diameter, with a doorway brilliant in colouring like a rude imitation of the stucco work of primitive Egyptians. The doorway was ample – six feet high and six feet wide, with a neat, arched approach. Plastered partitions divided the interior into segments of circles. One division before the wide doorway was intended as a hall of audience; behind the gaily decorated partition was the family bedchamber; to the right were segments of the circle devoted to the children. Huge refuse heaps of cow dung outside testified to the large herds of cattle at the chief's disposal.[4]

Two of Nyaika's sisters, Komuntali and Kibundabunda, who were themselves chiefs in Bulera and Butanda respectively, now plotted against him. Sending for another brother, Ndahura Mushuga, who was also in Busongora, they attempted to raise a rebellion under his leadership. Nyaika, however, learned of the plot and prepared a counterplan. Several of his loyal chiefs went at his command to Mushuga, pretending to offer their support which he gladly accepted. When the rival armies clashed at Kasunga, rather more than twenty miles east-south-east of Fort Portal as the crow flies, Mushuga's recent recruits betrayed him. The rebel force was defeated and Mushaga himself, together with his nephew, Bulemu, was captured and killed. In all, sixty men lost their lives in the fighting.

Kabuzi, a nephew of Mushuga and Nyaika, had promised to help the former in his campaign and was busy enlisting the aid of other princes in Busongora when the rival armies met. He was consequently too late to intervene in the battle which proved fatal to Mushuga's hopes. Some time afterwards, however, he attacked Nyaika's headquarters in the latter's absence, capturing 500 head of cattle and burning down his uncle's house. Whatever the plans of his aunts may have been Kabuzi made no attempt to supplant his uncle, contenting himself with what was little more than a raid. Nyaika for his part attempted no reprisals and it seems probable that at this stage the princes of Busongora were too strong to be challenged in their own territory. On the other hand, Nyaika's support in northern Toro seems at all times to have been unwavering. When, therefore, Kabuzi, emboldened by his earlier success, led another expedition against Nyaika some months later the result was a reversal of the previous campaign. The two armies met at Kanyanyange and Kabuzi was defeated and killed, together with several other Babito princes and one hundred fighting men on both sides.

Nyaika's great success worried some of the other Babito princes in Busongora who feared that he might try to restore the authority over their country which Kaboyo had once exercised. Under the leadership of Kato, Nyaika's brother, they made their way to Nkore where Kato, relying on his earlier friendship with Rukongyi, asked Mutambuka for assistance. It is difficult to date these events accurately, but if one follows Kasagama's chronology the visit to Nkore must have taken place in 1870 or early 1871. Karugire makes no specific mention of these events and if Kasagama's date is correct, Kato's request followed hard upon Mutambuka's disastrous intervention in the struggle for the succession in Bunyoro between Kabarega and Kabugumire. The army sent by the Mugabe to assist Kabugumire had been almost wiped out, after which Mutambuka had refused to give further help.[5] It is surprising, therefore, that the Mugabe should have been willing to assist in further escapades of a similar character so soon after the Bunyoro debacle. On the other hand, he may have thought an expedition to Toro a less hazardous undertaking and one which might restore the morale of his people.

Whatever Mutambuka's reasons the expedition he now authorized produced mixed results. The route taken by the invaders once again lay through Busongora because of the support which the Babito princes could count upon in that region. But the army was unable to unseat Nyaika, if that was its aim, and the Banyankore suffered heavy casualties. According to Kasagama they seized several hundred head of cattle and also established some sort of overlordship over Busongora. This is probably an over-statement, however, though Mutambuka undoubtedly had an interest in Busongora arising out of the marriage of his son, Bacwa, to a Mubito princess of that region, Kiboga, who was to play an important role in Toro's affairs in the late 1870s.

Kato was not disheartened by this setback. If Mutambuka's aid had proved inadequate there was still hope in the support of Kabaka Mutesa of Buganda. Mutesa himself was no greater warrior than Mutambuka, but his country was more powerful than Nkore. The Kabaka had already supported Kabarega's successful bid for power in Bunyoro, and Baganda forces had more recently waged war on the Sesse Islanders. In 1871, according to both Kasagama and Kaggwa,[6] Mutesa acceded to Kato's request and appointed Mukasa, the *Pokino* (chief) of Buddu, to lead a large army into Busongora. Mutesa put himself at the head of another expedition which was intended to reinforce Mukasa but which was diverted into a raid on Bunyoro.

Mukasa's expedition met with considerable success in its early stages. In their first encounter with the supporters of Nyaika the Baganda were victorious and Nyaika fled westward to take refuge on the slopes of the Ruwenzori Mountains while his goods and cattle were despatched to Butuku for safety. The Baganda followed up their victory by raiding Busongora. Then, sweeping northwards into Toro,[7] they enlisted the aid of rebellious Babito chiefs and pursued Nyaika from his hiding place until he was forced to retreat to Butuku.

With Nyaika out of the way Kato claimed the succession, but his triumph was brief. In spite of their military success the Baganda had suffered heavy losses. Several chiefs had been killed and a considerable number of soldiers had died from drinking impure water, as a boy who accompanied the expedition confirmed in conversation with H. M. Stanley only a few years later.[8] With his depleted forces Mukasa therefore returned at once to Buganda. Barely two months then elapsed before Kato's subjects rebelled and emissaries were sent to bring back Nyaika. Kato withdrew to Kibale, north-east of Lake George, where he subsequently died. Nyaika's return, meanwhile, was a source of satisfaction to the majority of the Batoro and Nyaika himself took what must have seemed two useful steps towards ensuring friendship with his neighbours when he married his daughter, Mukakyabana, to the newly enthroned Mukama Kabarega of Bunyoro, and another daughter to Mutambuka of Nkore. Busongora, however, was still giving trouble. First Isansa, the son of Kabuzi who had earlier fought against Nyaika, raised the standard of rebellion near Bugoye on the northern border of Busongora. A hastily arranged expedition led to his defeat but another Mubito prince, Kakoliole, briefly threatened the region round Bugoye only to be driven out by a Mukonjo chief. But the latter proved equally hostile to Nyaika; he was forced to lead another army against the rebels who were defeated after a struggle and their leader killed.

More serious trouble now beset the kingdom as a result, initially, of an act of foolish pride on Nyaika's part, although Toro would in any case have been swept up in the long run into events of a much wider significance. The roots of the problem lay in Toro's rebellion against the overlordship of Bunyoro. Hitherto a crisis had been averted by Bunyoro's preoccupation with events in other quarters, but the situation changed with the accession of the aggressive and warlike Kabarega. No love was lost between Nyaika and the Mukama in spite of the latter's marriage to Nyaika's daughter. From the outset Kabarega refused to acknowledge the independence of Toro and sent to Nyaika arrogant demands that he should come and do homage to his overlord. This summons Nyaika firmly rejected on the ground that his father, Kaboyo, had never paid tribute to Bunyoro and that all connection between Toro and Bunyoro had been severed by Kaboyo's rebellion. As a result of these hostile exchanges constant friction persisted along the borders between the two countries and petty raiding across the frontier was a normal feature of the early 1870s.

In this precarious situation some of Nyaika's men rashly entered the district of Mwenge, where Kabarega's cattle were grazing, and stole one of the Mukama's favourite cows. Nyaika refused a request for its return until two of his own cows, stolen by Kabarega, were also handed over. This momentary act of folly precipitated a series of campaigns which resulted in the temporary annihilation of Toro.

After the disturbances which had beset his reign it seems strange that Nyaika should have risked war for so trivial a matter. Yet even if pride overcame circumspection he had no reason to think that the outcome would be so dire. Kabarega was still a young man and had succeeded to the throne only after a severe struggle with his brother. He was not universally popular among his subjects and he had numerous external problems to occupy him. He was very conscious of the fact that he had come to the throne with the help of the Khartoum slave traders and he fully recognized their power and greed. Their continuing presence on his northern frontier was very disturbing and when, shortly after his accession, Sir Samuel Baker, acting on behalf of the Khedive of Egypt, arrived from the north in the company of some of the Khartoumers, Kabarega's suspicions were aroused. Although Baker claimed to represent a more respectable authority than his association with the slavers suggested, Kabarega did not trust him, and his distrust was fully justified when Baker declared Bunyoro to be an Egyptian protectorate. The Mukama resisted fiercely, whereupon Baker ceased to recognize Kabarega and instead acknowledged a rebellious kinsman, Ruyonga, as ruler of Bunyoro.[9] Kabarega was able to force Baker's withdrawal northward across the Nile but he remained conscious of a continuing threat from that quarter.

His misgivings were well-founded, for later in 1872 a mixed army consisting of some of Baker's men, reinforced by Acholi and some of Ruyonga's supporters, attacked and defeated Kabarega who was forced to seek refuge at Kibero on Lake Albert. About the same time Mutesa sent an army of 6000 Baganda to invade southern Bunyoro in the belief, encouraged by Baker, that Kabarega had blocked Baker's plan to trade with Buganda.[10] On 1 April 1873 Baker surrendered his office as representative of the Khedive, but before doing so he sent further reinforcements to assist Ruyonga and to install a garrison in a stockade opposite the islands in the Nile which Ruyonga used as his stronghold.[11]

News of Kabarega's problems must have reached Nyaika who, in spite of the Mukama's bluster, could hardly have expected him to leave his headquarters in Mparo to travel south to Toro at a time when his northern borders appeared in imminent danger of attack. But that is what Kabarega did. It has been suggested that the Mukama's aim was to protect his trade with the Zanzibaris because the prospect of developing a northern trade down the Nile was now threatened by his unfriendly relations with the Khartoumers.[12] This may indeed have been a subsidiary reason for his action; but the southern trade route which was known to run from Kabarega's capital to Karagwe, avoiding the territory of his rival in Buganda,[13] passed through Mwenge and Kitagwenda, some distance to the east of Nyaika's dominions, and while Nyaika may have been in a position to threaten the route there is no evidence of his having done so.

Without question Kabarega's main aim in attacking Toro was to recover the territories lost to Bunyoro during the reigns of his weaker predecessors. Kabarega was a man of tremendous energy and ambition and was determined that the family rivalries which had divided the empire should be stamped out. His first step, however, was not intended as a war of reoccupation because he still lacked the means to put such a plan into effect. Instead he attempted to overawe his opponents by a demonstration of ruthless power. Accounts of the outcome of this first raid differ, depending upon the source. That the Banyoro, assisted by Bakedi, penetrated deep into Toro is certain, but while Fisher says that they carried off thousands of cattle[14] Kasagama claims that they were defeated and driven back. In response to Kabarega's further call to pay tribute Nyaika now boldly refused, and seeing that the Mukama threatened to repeat the attack he turned for support to Mutambuka, ruler of Nkore.[15] The Mugabe again responded to the appeal of his kinsman by marriage, a relationship which both he and his successor, Ntare V, always appeared anxious to honour, but the force he despatched arrived to find that Nyaika had already died of smallpox.[16] The Banyankore therefore withdrew and played no part in the later struggle with Bunyoro.

Nyaika's reign had been a short one, possible no more than five or six years in length, and had been largely taken up in a struggle for survival. The date of his death cannot be fixed with accuracy. If Kasagama's chronology is to be accepted he must have died no later than 1872. On the other hand, at the end of 1875 Stanley had news of Toro – or Gambaragara as he called it – from natives of the region who thought Nyaika was still the ruler.[17] These informants may not, it is true, have been in Toro for some time and if Mutambuka was still ruling in Nkore at the time of Nyaika's death then Kasagama's chronology would appear to be the safest to follow. The best estimate which can be made is that Nyaika died between 1872 and 1875. In one respect at least he maintained the traditions which his father had brought from Bunyoro. Kasagama lists certain chiefs to whom Nyaika granted the right to wear the crown of colobus monkey skin. No reason is given for the awards, though it seems likely that they were made for loyalty and assistance during his years of struggle.

Nyaika was not an old man when he died. Indeed, there were

those who firmly believed that his death was due to witchcraft, and his sister, Byanjeru, took vengeance upon a number of people who, she claimed, had been involved in magical activities against their ruler. The result of these suspicions was that the country became more divided than ever, a situation which was in no way helped by the fact that Nyaika had left fourteen sons to contest the succession, though several were too young to be actively involved in the struggle. Olimi IV Makubire was the first to be recognized, but almost at once Kalikura, one of Nayaika's Mukonjo supporters, urged another prince, Mukarusa by name, to seize control of Busongora, which he was able to do because of the weakness of Mukabire. The latter seems to have commanded relatively little support in any district, and when his country was again invaded by forces sent by Kabarega many of the Batoro joined the invaders or fled to the mountains for safety. Another chief, Rwomire, betrayed Mukabire to the leader of the invaders, thereby ensuring his own personal safety after their victory.[18]

Forced to surrender, Mukabire was taken to Bunyoro where he remained in captivity, closely guarded at Kabarega's command, until he was able to make his escape in 1893 or 1894 when Buganda, assisted by British forces, launched the attack upon Bunyoro which was to destroy Kabarega's power. Mukabire then made his way to Busoga where he received messengers urging him to return to Toro, but he died in Buganda before he was able to reach his homeland.

In the meantime Toro's position had declined still further, though Kasagama's account differs from that contained in Fisher's book. The latter tends to conflate a number of events[19] dealt with individually and in more detail by Kasagama. According to Kasagama, although the Banyoro forces had been defeated by Mukarusa when they attempted to invade Busongora, they laid waste most of Toro and then withdrew. Even then, however, there was no assurance of a lasting peace. Another brother of Mukabire, Isingoma, briefly succeeded him but, unable to muster support, was compelled to give way to yet another brother, Rububi. Rububi then ruled for a brief period without being threatened by Bunyoro, but his good fortune did not last. In 1873 (if Kasagama is to be believed, though it could have been as late as 1878), Kabarega launched another and more devastating attack against Toro under the leadership of the *saza* (county) chief of Bugangaizi, Kikukule, and Rububi fled. On this occasion even the redoubtable Mukonjo chief, Kalikura, surrendered and, according to Fisher,[20] was put to death by Kabarega's order for having had the audacity to challenge the authority of one of royal descent. It was probably during this campaign that Mukarusa, too, was taken prisoner and put to death.[21] Due to treachery some of the royal children were surrendered to Rosongoza, whom Kikukule had left to carry on the campaign after his own initial victories. Others were more fortunate, among them Nyaika's young son, Kasagama, who with some of his brothers and sisters was taken for safety to Nkore.

In Nkore the children passed some years contentedly until Kiboga, the mother of Mugabe Ntare V, decided to take a hand. Kiboga was herself a Mubito princess from Busongora and her intervention on this and on a number of other occasions in the affairs to Toro did little to stabilize that strife-torn country. She may well have been a close relation of Rububi for it was in his interests that she acted both now and later. Kasagama himself said that Kiboga sent for the children, but, whether from prescience or other form of natural caution, his eldest sisters urged him not to accept the invitation and instead went themselves with their attendants. One of the latter returned to report that the girls had been killed, at which Kasagama and his other relations – brothers, sisters and cousins – together with their friends, fled the country. Some made their way to Bunyoro, while Kasagama took refuge in Buganda.[22] Kiboga's motive in attempting to kill the royal children was presumably to dispose of potential rivals to Rububi.

After the Bunyoro onslaught Rububi himself appears to have taken refuge in Buganda and it would seem that for a time the Banyoro forces remained in Toro. Then Namuyonjo Kakende, another prince who had fled to Buganda, successfully appealed to Kabaka Mutesa for armed assistance to enable him to return to his country. The Kabaka's response was in keeping with his practice of alternately supporting and attacking Kabarega, for Mutesa was anxious to exploit Bunyoro's weakness when it was expedient to do so but rallied to his rival's assitance when the threat from Egypt cast its shadow over Buganda. He therefore placed a large force at Kakende's disposal. The army marched into Toro where it met with immediate success, forcing the Banyoro to withdraw and enabling Kakende to claim the government of the country. Both Kaggwa and Kasagama say that these events took place in 1875,[23] but Stanley, who was in Buganda in that year, refers only to the *katikkiro's* (a Luganda word meaning initially, 'chief counsellor', but later acquiring the meaning 'chief minister') successful raid on Busongora which took place during Nyaika's reign,[24] so that Kakende's invasion almost certainly occurred at a later date.

The Baganda who had made possible the ejection of the Banyoro were not prepared to remain indefinitely in Toro, and when they returned in triumph to their homes Kakende went with them, leaving two of his supporters in charge of affairs on his behalf. The reason for Kakende's behaviour is difficult to ascertain. From Kasagama's *Memoir* it would seem that the people of Toro accepted him as their ruler and fully expected him to come back to claim the throne without much delay. It was, therefore, perhaps discretion, rather than ambition, which compelled him to act as he did. When, after some time, he still failed to return, the people of Toro sought a new leader and appointed yet another brother, Katera, who was confident that he would be able to control most of Toro although the Banyoro still occupied a portion of the country.

Once again Kiboga, the mother of Ntare V of Nkore, intervened. She now sent messengers urging her protégé, Rububi, to return from exile and seize power. Rububi responded to her appeal, and making his way to Toro was quickly able to overthrow Katera, but he in turn was supplanted in 1879 or 1880 by Kakende, who had again enlisted the aid of troops from Buganda.[25] Kakende was not to rule for long, however, for Kabarega determined once again to try to bring Toro under his control. Two of his leading generals, Kikukule and Nyakamatura, were given the task of overthrowing the Toro pretender and with their professional armies they drove Kakende out of his country. He took refuge in Nkore but then moved to Buganda where he died in the early 1880s.

Busongora remained unconquered, but sustained resistance in Toro was now at an end. Kabarega appointed his maternal uncle, Ruburwa, as chief of Toro,[26] but the government of the conquered territory was mainly in the hands of the Mukama's generals. These were for the most part new men, but new men were not unknown in the Banyoro hierarchy. It was the circumstances in which they took office and the system they operated which were new – and important because of their novelty. The hostility shown by most of the Babito princes to Kabarega's succession and the difficulty he had encountered from their military opposition had convinced the Mukama that the old way of doing things must be changed. His dependence upon provincial levies, many of them raised and captained by princes, acting as *saza* chiefs, who might themselves be claimants to the throne, left the ruler in a permanently precarious position which the aura of monarchy could not of itself overcome. The theoretical loyalty of all the lesser chiefs to the Mukama, and their ultimate dependence upon him for the authority they exercised, had proved illusory in practice.

The struggle for the succession had at least demonstrated to Kabarega who were his friends and who his enemies, and while it was not immediately practicable to remove all the latter he was certainly able to replace some of them, and at the same time to build up a counterweight to the others. Although it was necessary to permit a number of *saza* chiefs who had opposed his succession to continue in office, Kabarega developed a professional army to offset their powers. Fortunately for his plans the hostility shown him by most of the Babito was not shared by the commoner classes. So, while continuing to rely on those chiefs who, like Nyakamatura, had been unswerving in their loyalty, he sought out and gave important military commands to commoners of proven ability. Kikukule was such a man who, in addition to being given command of a regiment, and sometimes overall command of an army as in the two campaigns against Toro already described, was made *saza* chief of the important border district of Bugangaizi. This area was formerly part of the heartland of Bunyoro but had recently become a frontier region, constantly harassed by Buganda. An even more striking appointment was that of Ireeta, one of the leaders of the defeated Nkore army sent to assist Kabugumire against Kabarega in the succession struggle. Although on the opposing side in that campaign Ireeta so impressed Kabarega that he offered him service in Bunyoro, and not only gave him command of a regiment but also, after the conquest of the frontier district of Mboga – beyond the Semliki River – in the 1880s, made him *saza* chief; he does not, however, appear to have been there when Stanley passed through in 1889.[27]

Kabarega's regiments, *bitongole*, about ten in number and each between 1000 and 2000 strong, were themselves an innovation in that they provided the Mukama for the first time with a standing army, the members of which were called *barasura*.[28] Their permanency contrasted with the temporary character of the provincial levies which consisted mainly of civilians in arms. They were manned for the most part by Banyoro, but Kabarega did not hesitate to enlist foreigners into his army – Madi, Langi and Acholi among them. Nor was he averse to employing Khartoumers to train his men in the use of firearms, for a high proportion of the *barasura* were armed with muskets while some of their leaders carried weapons of even greater precision.

It took some time to build this military force into its final form, although it seems that Kabarega started work upon it immediately after his accession and that from the early 1870s it played an important part in the affairs of the empire. Regiments were stationed in strategic parts of the country. Those located near the centre, like the one commanded by the great military leader Rwabudongo, acted as a protective force for the Mukama himself, but when needed were available for more distant campaigns, as for example in Butuku in 1889.[29] The regiments in more remote districts ensured that *saza* chiefs should not be in a position, either individually or by banding together, to threaten their overlord. The loyalty of the generals was itself guaranteed by a number of factors. For the most part they owed their positions to the Mukama and they had no dynastic claims to office. They were, too, required to attend at reasonable intervals upon the Mukama, while both they and their Banyoro followers appear to have been bound to Kabarega by ties of friendship and respect. In time of war they were expected to hand over their booty to the Mukama but a generous portion was returned to them. In time of peace they tended to live off the land, sometimes cultivating it themselves, sometimes pillaging *saza* chiefs whose loyalty was suspect and to whose authority they acted as a useful counterweight. In this way, although the traditional system of administration seemed to be still in force, the chiefs, except for those who were the nominees of Kabarega, found many of their former powers curtailed.

When the *barasura* invaded enemy territory they plundered without restraint, and the Batoro suffered as heavily as any of those who came into contact with them. The princes who successively attempted to assert their control over Toro were seen by Kabarega as supreme examples of the aristocratic threat which endangered the unity of the empire and must therefore be driven from the country to make way for an army of occupation. The presence of these invaders was naturally unwelcome to the inhabitants. The rule of Kaboyo and his descendants may have aroused mixed sentiments in the hearts of the population, but the predatory *barasura* were loved by none.

The conquest of Busongora by the armies of Bunyoro took place in the early 1880s. This region had remained largely independent of the rest of Toro throughout the preceding decade and had experienced considerable unrest as a result of the rivalries of the Babito princes who lived there. In 1881 one of them, Kaihura, tried to extend his control across the Kazinga Channel to the strip of low-lying land which forms the northern marches of Bunyaruguru. His aim was to seize additional grazing land and new sources of tribute, and possibly to obtain a more effective control of the salt trade. The Banyaruguru put up a vigorous resistance and he was driven out of the country. Making his way to Nkore he asked his sister, Kiboga, to intercede with her son, Mugabe Ntare V, on his behalf. Ntare was greatly attracted by the prospect of acquiring more cattle and agreed to provide an army to assist Kaihura. The raiding force invaded Bunyaruguru, but although Kaihura was able to seize control of the country the Banyankore failed to find the cattle for which they had hoped. They therefore crossed the Kazinga Channel into Busongora and looked for loot there, Kaihura accompanying them and re-establishing himself in the vicinity of the salt lakes.[30]

The withdrawal of the Banyankore must have been followed within a few years by the decisive attack upon Busongora by the armies of Bunyoro led by Ireeta. The Banyoro seized control of the salt lakes and the workers at the lakes, including the two thousand inhabitants of the village of Katwe, found themselves compelled to labour for new and harsher masters. The trade was then diverted from its southerly routes to meet the demands of Bunyoro. Ireeta did not, however, push the campaign further. The Bakanjo to the west of Katwe remained unmolested and although Ireeta left another general, Rukara, in charge of the region when he himself went off to fight in Mboga, Kaihura appears to have been able to hang on to the spit of land projecting into Lake Edward to the south-east of Katwe. Stanley, who passed through the area in 1889, said that Kaihura had contrived to keep his independence and that his settlement consisted of eighty-one large huts, with an abundance of sheep and goats.[31] Kakule, too – the leader of the salt traders of Lake Edward, a well-built, dark-featured man – refused to submit to the Banyoro invaders, and although deprived of his livelihood pursued an independent existence on his island strongholds in the lake. Skilled in handling canoes, his men were reasonably secure from any attack from the northern shore. It was, however, a great relief to all those who had come to depend so completely upon the salt trade when Stanley's arrival caused Rukara to take flight and enabled them to make up for the backlog in their activities. Their customers to the south were also delighted to renew their stocks after being starved of salt throughout the occupation of Katwe by the *barasura* although their good fortune was short-lived because Rukara returned to seize control after Stanley's departure.[32]

Marching in an easterly direction Stanley came to Lake George, where he again found that the salt traders had withdrawn to their islands to seek safety from the *barasura* while Rukara's forces had denuded the mainland to the west of the lake of cattle and all movable goods. Wherever he went Stanley found evidence of the devastation created by the Banyoro armies, from Bwamba on the northern slopes of the Ruwenzoris to Lake George, and Lugard, who came to Toro two years later, made similar observations. Kabarega's forces made no serious attempt to administer the country but simply raided the population, driving away their cattle and seizing their crops, reducing the Batoro to destitution and filling them with terror until they were afraid even to respond to Lugard's friendly overtures.

Kitagwenda, to the east of Lake George, was able to escape these sufferings. When Stanley arrived there in 1889 he found the country ruled by Ruigi as it had been when he was in the neighbourhood in 1876. Ruigi had never owed allegiance to Toro, but he had, like his predecessors, maintained an ill-defined, sometimes tributary, relationship with Bunyoro. Fortunately Kabarega had found too many problems elsewhere and had largely ignored Kitagwenda. Although forced to keep an apprehensive eye upon his more powerful neighbours Ruigi had therefore been able to keep his country safe by the judicious payment of tribute to Kabarega and Ntare simultaneously. Kitagwenda had remained prosperous amid the surrounding turmoil, with a plentiful supply of food – millet, beans and potatoes, with bananas for beer. By permitting traders to pass freely through the country *en route* for Bunyoro, Ruigi escaped the anger of Kabarega and benefited from the trade himself. The breakdown in the salt trade hit his people hard, however, because they had developed an important role as entrepreneurs, due to their proximity to Lake George. In spite of this setback Kitagwenda in general remained something of a haven amid the conflicts of the 1870s and 1880s, and as an agricultural country was much less seriously affected than were some of her neighbours by the epidemic of rinderpest which destroyed the herds of western Uganda in the later 1880s.

For the remnants of Kaboyo's kingdom, however, the 1880s marked the period of darkest night. Kabarega had no mercy upon the inhabitants of the rebel state, and even the peasantry who had benefited little enough from Kaboyo himself and still less in the years of civil war which followed his death, looked back to those days as a time of relative comfort compared with the tragic years of the Banyoro occupation.

III · The Kingdom Revived

The reincarnation of Toro came not as a result of internal efforts but as a by-product of British activity in the lake region. On 3 September 1888 the Imperial British East Africa Company received from Queen Victoria a royal charter authorizing it to promote trade, commerce and good government in those parts of the East African mainland and the offshore islands where it had been granted, or might subsequently be granted, concessions by the local rulers. The Company was also to do all in its power to put an end to the slave trade.[1]

The charter's reference to 'Grants, Concessions, Agreements and Treaties' as determining the nature of the Company's activities reflects the concern felt by some of the legal experts in the Foreign Office about the way in which relations between European and African states were developing. During the Berlin West African Conference of 1884–5, the British Lord Chancellor, Lord Selborne, had seen that Britain's interests were best served by the minimum of official involvement necessary to protect the lawful commercial activities of her citizens in various parts of the African continent. In the face of strong German opposition he had therefore insisted that the declaration of a protectorate by a European Power over any part of Africa committed that Power only to controlling the external relations of the protected state. Reluctantly the German Chancellor, Bismarck, had accepted this interpretation although he greatly resented Britain's arbitrary claims to a special role in areas where she had a minimum of representation.[2] Subsequently, however, although Germany assumed that her protectorates remained foreign territories under German suzerainty, she claimed that all persons within such protectorates, irrespective of nationality, must be subject to German jurisdiction. She went on to claim that such jurisdiction did not derive from the native chiefs of the areas concerned, although in some cases jurisdiction over the native population might be left by treaty in the hands of the native chiefs on grounds of expediency.

The British Prime Minister, Lord Salisbury, protested that such an interpretation was contrary to international law, which stated that the right of jurisdiction over persons found in any territory belonged only to the Power which was entitled to rights of territorial sovereignty.[3] This praiseworthy concern for the sovereign rights of African rulers (and, it should be added, for the non-involvement of the British Government in responsibility for unpromising African territories) left unanswered the question of who should exercise jurisdiction over foreign nationals in a state whose relations with foreigners were apparently controlled by a Protecting Power. An amendment was clearly needed to the Foreign Jurisdiction Act of 1843, which authorized the British Crown to exercise jurisdiction over British subjects in a foreign country subject to the approval of the government of the country concerned.

At the very time at which the I.B.E.A. Company's Charter was under consideration, legal arguments were in fact developing over the scope of a new Foreign Jurisdiction bill.[4] In the light of those arguments the Company's Charter was warily drafted in terms which ensured that the Company's representatives should not offend against international law. The Company also thoughtfully provided its agents with specimen treaty forms which catered for the cession by a native ruler of 'all his sovereign rights' to the Company, so that no one would be in a position to question any action which the Company's representatives might take. The fact that the Company had been given a charter at all, after years of fruitless importunity, was a clear indication of Salisbury's growing recognition of the strategic importance of the Nile Valley in relation to the Suez Canal route to the East.

The Company's immediate problems were of a practical rather than of a legal character. Confused in its objectives and under-capitalized, it was essential that the Company should open up a profitable trade as quickly as possible if it were to survive. The only hope was to tap the ivory supplies which lay deep in the interior of the continent. A footing had already been established in Buganda eleven years earlier by representatives of the Church Missionary Society and they had been followed shortly afterwards by French missionaries of the White Fathers Missions. The presence of ivory, combined with the attractions of working in a country which, as numerous explorers had insisted, possessed a well-organized government and a large population anxious to acquire manufactured goods, made Buganda the Company's obvious goal, and Captain F. D. Lugard was despatched on a mission into the interior in 1890.

One important obstacle appeared to have been removed from Lugard's path. Earlier in the year the line which since 1886 had divided the German from the British sphere of influence in East Africa had been extended westward across Lake Victoria along the 1° North line of latitude as far as the 30° East line of longitude, thus incorporating most of what is now Uganda within the British sphere of influence. It was hoped, therefore, that there would be no cause for a clash of interests between the I.B.E.A. Company and the representatives of Germany.

Unfortunately for the Company's hopes of peaceful development, divisions had recently occurred in the formerly powerful state of Buganda as a result of which the new Kabaka, Mwanga, had been forced to flee from the country. His rivals in the kingdom had been aided by the rampant Kabarega who had warmed to the prospect of fulfilling his hopes of converting Bunyoro's most powerful opponent into a client state and had willingly sent armed assistance. With the help of some of the Christian converts among his subjects, who had been driven from the country by rival interests in the wake of the Kabaka, Mwanga had been able to recover his throne. But rebellious elements still threatened him and the hosts of Kabarega lurked menacingly on his north-western frontier.

Into this uneasy situation Lugard marched, with a handful of troops and an abundance of determination. He was quick to appreciate the weakness of his position, however. All around him were thousands of armed men capable at any moment of renewing the civil war. His assessment of the position coincided with that of the missionaries who had already concluded that, whatever the personal merits of Mwanga – and they may not have appeared very numerous – their only hope of continuing their work in the country lay in supporting the Kabaka. Provided that he could induce Mwanga to come to an agreement which would promote the Company's objectives, it was in Lugard's interest too to throw his weight in the balance on the Kabaka's side. It was obvious, however, that a member of Buganda's royal line, however straitened his circumstances, would not set his seal to one of the Company's ready-made treaties. Nor, on the advice of rival missionaries, who saw in their own identification with the Kabaka's interests the best hopes of the survival of their cause, was Mwanga likely to be deceived by Lugard into making concessions to the Company which might prove detrimental to his own position. The treaty which Mwanga signed in December 1890, therefore, simply recognized the Company's suzerainty, although the Kabaka did agree to place the assessment and collection of the country's taxes under a committee of finance to be presided over by the Company's Resident so that the revenue could be most satisfactorily employed for the protection and development of the country.

Having progressed so far Lugard next turned to the problem of assisting Mwanga to destroy the rebels who, along with Kabarega, were threatening the north-western frontier. In conjunction with a large army from Buganda the Company's small military force soon inflicted a heavy if temporary setback upon the Banyoro legions and their allies. It was obvious to Lugard, however, that any prospect of a profitable trade in Uganda depended upon the restoration of order throughout the whole region, in Buganda as well as in Bunyoro, and to do this two things were necessary; first, more forces must be placed at his own disposal, and second, there must be a vast reduction in the number of firearms in the hands of Africans. Any attempt to reduce the number of firearms in Buganda would, however, require a great deal of guile, or a great deal of force.[5]

One possibility of acquiring such a force appeared to Lugard to lie in enlisting the aid of the Sudanese troops left by Emin Pasha in the vicinity of the western shores of Lake Albert when he withdrew from the governorship of the Egyptian Equatorial Province in 1889. These men were now cut off from all hope of returning to their homeland by the armies of the Mahdi which occupied the Sudan and even threatened Egypt itself. To get in touch with these troops, led by Selim Bey, would involve a journey to the west of Uganda, but the most direct route, which lay through Bunyoro itself, was deemed to be impracticable. Reliable informants claimed that there were no food supplies and that the region was criss-crossed by rivers and swamps. An alternative, more southerly and more circuitous, path must be found, and in this way Toro came to play an important part in Lugard's plans.[6]

The gallant captain was quick to see the advantages to be gained by accepting circumstances as he found them. 'It is, in my opinion,' he wrote,

> a most urgent and useful task to construct a road (that is of course merely to pass along, make treaties, and build small forts at intervals) along the route from Buddu to the South of the Albert Lake. By this I think we should divert the trade of Unyoro &c. which is supposed to go to Kafru the capital of Karagwe. . . . We should also have, perhaps, as

good a line towards Wadelai . . . as any which could be made. Thus goods would come across Victoria to Buddu, thence direct to Kavalli and thence Northwards to the Sudan. . . . It would be the line I have always wished to hold, to check the import of arms and powder from the South. It would be more or less conterminous (for purposes of taxation and customs, observations &c.) with the German boundary, a point I think of great importance. . . . It is the direct route to the salt supplying district, and, if we can hold this, we can exchange the salt for all the products of Uganda and the surrounding countries. It is the gold-field of this part of Africa.[7]

These ideas were indicative of Lugard's fertile invention rather than of any clearcut plan, but the future became more discernible on 5 June 1891 when Zachariah Kisingiri, a Protestant Muganda chief who had attached himself enthusiastically to Lugard, brought to him two men. The elder was Yafeti Byakuyamba, a Munyoro member of the ruling dynasty who had fled from Mwenge to escape the anger of Kabarega and who had become a Christian while in exile in Buganda. The younger was a youth who proved to be Kasagama, son of Nyaika, the former ruler of Toro. These men presented themselves as potentially valuable agents for the promotion of Lugard's campaign to establish an administrative system in Uganda which would assist the Company's commercial aims, for they claimed that they could win the population of Toro away from Kabarega whom the people detested.[8] When, therefore, Lugard set out westward, Kasagama and Yafeti went with him.

The route lay through Nkore, where Lugard made a treaty with a representative of Ntare V of Nkore under the terms of which the Mugabe recognized the Company's representative and undertook to try to prevent the import of arms and ammunition into the British sphere and to stop Europeans, other than the Company's representatives, from settling in his country. On the strength of this slight agreement with a ruler he had never met Lugard was pleased to record that Nkore had been 'Annexed by the present of a load of cloth!'[9] The prospects for Yafeti and Kasagama seemed distinctly limited.

Kaihura, whose hold over Bunyaruguru was still resented by its inhabitants though they dared not oppose him through fear of his ally, Ntare, welcomed Lugard and his forces. Having held on to the southern shore of the Kazinga Channel he was anxious to see the salt trade to the south re-opened. So, too, were Kakule and his people who, because of the diversion of the trade to Bunyoro, had been living in considerable poverty in crowded lake-side villages consisting of houses which were no more than grass bivouacs. At once fifty or more large canoes were placed at Lugard's disposal, each big enough to hold thirty or forty men though made of the thinnest planks, sewn together and calked with grass. Unopposed, the flotilla crossed the narrow neck of the western Kazinga Channel to the spit of land on which now stands the game lodge. The armed forces of Rukara, Kabarega's general, had boldly shouted challenges across the water the previous evening, but now withdrew north-eastward. The salt workers, too, fled before the advancing caravan and Lugard entered the empty village of Katwe to find cooking fires still burning. Kakule's men, seeing the way clear, swarmed across the channel and began to load their canoes with salt, fighting and rushing like madmen to seize again the important commodity of which they had been deprived for so long.

Lugard's success still left the future of Toro unsettled. Kabarega's forces lurked in the vicinity, while the people of Busongora and Toro watched fearfully to see the outcome of the struggle. Lugard therefore decided to build a stockade to control the salt trade and called it Fort George. Perched on a narrow neck of bare, sunburnt rock between Lakes Edward and Katwe it was virtually impregnable, but Lugard knew full well that even to hold on to Katwe would be impossible without the aid of Selim Bey's troops. A small garrison, surrounded by enemies, would inevitably be starved into submission.

In recent years an adventurer named Karakwanzi had taken advantage of the unsettled state of Busongora to attract to himself a following of purposeful men with whose aid he had made himself effective ruler of most of the country to the west of Katwe, extending even beyond the Semliki River. He now came to Katwe, with a large following, offering to cooperate with Lugard and to provide guides to show him the route round the western flank of the Ruwenzori Mountains to the region where Selim was thought to have his camp. Kasagama's first reaction to the arrival of these reinforcements was one of pleasure, but later he became suspicious and resentful of Karakwanzi because the latter claimed to be supreme ruler of a large part of Busongora. Nor was he reassured by the evidence of Lugard's observations which confirmed that the energetic little man was widely accepted as overlord by the inhabitants of all the country around the south-western limits of the Ruwenzoris.[10] Whatever Kasagama's pretensions, however, former rights meant little amid the uncertainty occasioned by Kabarega's conquests; only effective military power counted, and fortunately for Karakwanzi, Kabarega had been satisfied to seize the salt without bothering to annex the country further westward.

Lugard's expedition to the west of the mountains failed to make contact with Selim Bey. He therefore decided to try the eastern route through Toro itself. Following this path he could at least test the reaction of the Batoro to the return of Kasagama. Rukara and his *barasura* offered little resistance to his advance but the Basongora and Batoro were too afraid of Kabarega's reprisals to come forward boldly to greet Kasagama. Their feelings must in any case have been mixed. For much of the late 1860s and 1870s Busongora had been the seat of rebellion against whoever set himself up as ruler of Toro, and while the chiefs, divided in their loyalties, were sometimes triumphant, sometimes cast down, the people as a whole suffered continually from the endemic struggle. Toro, too, had been a constant battlefield, so that the memories of Nyaika's reign could not of themselves have caused the hearts of the people to beat with enthusiasm for the return of Nyaika's son. Yet the rapacious years of Kabarega had brought them even greater grief, and they were now left scarcely knowing how to respond to the news that Kasagama was once more among them.

Until this time Kasagama himself had done little to impress his presence on the country. A large, physically powerful youth, he was yet too young to have the stamp of leadership on him, and during the march westward it was Yafeti whom Lugard had consulted rather than his young protégé. Nor was Kasagama equipped to assert himself in Lugard's dominant presence. That Lugard took such pains to reintroduce Kasagama to Toro is not, therefore, easily explained. No doubt he hoped for a more positive response to the appeal of Kasagama's name from the Batoro than was in the event forthcoming, but his earlier talk of restoring the young man to power was quickly modified to suit the Company's interests more closely. On reaching the Mubuku River, which marked the frontier between Busongora and Toro, and without waiting to test the reaction of the Toro people further, he – to use Kasagama's own phrase – 'Wrote me an agreement'; this describes the situation perfectly.

The agreement which Kasagama was required to accept was no confidence trick such as Carl Peters employed to induce some ignorant chief to sign away his, or more probably his people's, birthright. Lugard was perfectly clear in his own mind that Kasagama owed everything to the Company. Whatever his reception might in due course be among his own people he would not have been there to enjoy it without the Company's aid. The Company's right to Toro was, therefore, in Lugard's view absolute. Effectively it was based upon conquest. Kasagama's role was simply that of the Company's agent, his hereditary association with the country being nothing more than a useful instrument to win over the goodwill of the people. The treaty to which Lugard and Kasagama gave their consent on 14 August 1891, therefore, involved no transfer of land or power to the Company but was simply a recognition of the Company's rightful status. Kasagama was required to acknowledge that he had been 'made King of Toro by the British' and that 'Toro and all its dependencies including Busongora and Bukonju, and the countries which may come under my rule, hereafter, are entirely under the British Company, and I and my successors hold ourselves bound to obey the orders and instructions of the Company's representatives in all matters whatsoever.' He would also do all in his power to prevent the import of arms and powder into Toro or any other of the Company's territories. He would recognize the Company's exclusive right to the country's ivory supplies (the salt supplies were already a Company monopoly) and would endeavour to pay the expenses of any garrison required to defend the country as well as footing the bill for development from the country's own resources. If any doubt might then remain as to who was in control, Lugard, who had drafted the agreement on the back of the Company's printed treaty form, went on to sign the printed copy after altering the words 'And has ceded to the Company all his sovereign rights' so that they read 'recognizes the Company's sovereign rights'.[11]

It is difficult to know what Kasagama made of the Agreement. There is no doubt, however, that for him the return to Toro was a reclamation of what he believed to be his of right. In any case, a treaty was premature. Lugard as yet stood only on the threshold of Toro. Although there had so far been little resistance to his advance it seemed more than likely that before long Kabarega would muster his forces and put up a fight, and Lugard had not yet made contact with Selim Bey. This he now decided to do. Leaving Kasagama and Yafeti to build a village in the vicinity of the fort he had started to construct on the borders of Toro – Fort Edward, he marched north. The country through which he passed was densely cultivated, but everyone had fled, the Banyoro invaders as well as any Batoro whom Rukara's soldiers had not killed or driven off in fetters to prevent them deserting to Kasagama.[12]

A little north of the site of the present Fort Portal Lugard concluded that there was little prospect of forcing Rukara to join battle with him. The fire from Lugard's Maxim gun had made the Banyoro fearful to stand and fight, and Rukara simply continued his withdrawal north-eastward to Mwenge. Giving up the pursuit, Lugard turned north-westward towards Lake Albert and Selim's encampment. Kabarega had sent urgent orders to his general, Ireeta, to intercept Lugard on his way to Butuku, but Ireeta was wary of a head-on encounter and Lugard's crossing of the Semliki River was accomplished with such speed that a night attack planned by the Banyoro against Lugard's camp on the east bank of the river misfired because he was already on the other side.

Beyond the Semliki Lugard was received with acclaim by villagers who had only recently been plundered of all their possessions by one of Kabarega's armies. Here Lugard assumed that he was beyond the boundaries of Bunyoro and certainly outside any region that might have had any affiliation with the old Kingdom of Toro, so he did not hesitate to inform the people that this was now British territory[13] under the terms of the Anglo-German Agreement of 1890 which rendered any claim made by Kabarega irrelevant. It was on the basis of that agreement, too, that Lugard invited Selim Bey to join the Company's service when he eventually met him on the heights above Lake Albert.

At this point Lugard's opportunism almost outran even his own generous interpretation of his purpose in the Lake Region. The attraction of seizing Wadelai, and thus making a name for himself as a military commander by paving the way for the recovery of the Sudan, was probably only thwarted by Selim's refusal to move northwards without orders from his former master, the Khedive of Egypt. With some reluctance Lugard noted that, 'For the Company's interests I think that probably it would be as well if Wadelai is left alone for the present. . . . Toro has yet to be settled and a series of stations built.' Philosophically he turned his face southward, and with Selim Bey and his Sudanese troops and followers, some 4000 in number, who were now committed to support the Company pending further orders from the Khedive, he began the return journey with the intention of establishing garrisons along what he believed to be the frontier of Toro. 'West of that line there would be peace and the British flag, East of it *war*,' he wrote.[14]

His choice of site for the first garrison, which he was to call Fort Wavertree, emphasized the importance of the strategic element in his thinking. Abandoning the Semliki Plain, he built the fort on the 5000-feet-high plateau dominating the open country of Butuku to the north, in the vicinity of Ireeta's own encampment. Ireeta himself, along with his army, had deserted the area at Lugard's approach. Here, as elsewhere, the Batoro who had suffered heavily under Kabarega's oppressive rule cautiously began to make contact with Lugard.[15] One of them, an elderly man who appeared to be a chief or spokesman, Lugard induced to build a village beside the fort where he would act as Kasagama's representative and be responsible for all matters concerning the natives of the region, a role which was also clearly explained to the Sudanese commander of the garrison lest he should take it upon himself to interfere.[16] Similar arrangements were subsequently made at each of the stockades which Lugard was to build, because he was anxious to keep the control of the Sudanese forces separate from the civil administration.[17] In the event Fort Wavertree quickly became the centre of a large African township, well laid-out and increasingly prosperous in an area where food was plentiful.

The site of the next stockade, Fort Lorne, some 15 miles

S.S.E. of Fort Wavertree, was on the southern border of Mwenge, near Butiti, on the main route to Kabarega's capital. The third stockade, Fort Kivari, 17 miles S.S.W. of Fort Lorne, effectively removed the need for Fort Edward as a defended site. The object of establishing the forts was not so much to define the boundary of Toro as to protect the trade routes which ran from Lake Victoria across Ankole and northward through Kitagwenda, passing well to the west of the defended line. It was to consolidate this position that Lugard was shortly to build two further stockades, Fort Ntara and Fort Grant, in Kitagwenda itself. Nor did he intend to accept this as the final boundary: it was his intention to take the offensive against Kabarega as soon as possible and to wheel the line of forts through a 90° arc from Fort Lorne. The defended frontier would then no longer run north–south, but east–west across the middle of Mwenge, roughly along the line of the present Mubende–Fort Portal road, and Toro would cease to be a frontier district.

With the west now reasonably secure from Kabarega, if not from the rapacity of the Sudanese stationed in the stockades to defend the country, a more detailed appraisal of the administrative problem could be made, and this Lugard proceeded to do in November 1891. Although he had good reports of Kasagama and Yafeti from many quarters he decided that the former would have his hands full settling Bunyangabo and Burahya. In spite of Kasagama's jealously of Karakwanzi, the little man had made such a good impression on Lugard that the latter determined to allow him to stay for the time being in the vicinity of Katwe. The salt lake would be exclusively administered by the Company, however, and so too would the rest of Busongora north-eastward from Katwe. The territory to the west and north-west of the salt lake would be left under the control of Karakwanzi though this was not intended to call into question Kasagama's claim to include the whole of Busongora within the Toro Kingdom at some future date. Any decision about putting this extension of the young man's authority into effect would be taken in the light of Kasagama's performance in what Lugard described as Toro Proper,[18] that is, in Bunyangabo and Burahya.

Although he believed that Kitagwenda had in time past formed part of the Kingdom of Toro, Lugard initially decided that it should be administered by the Company so as to free the region from Kabarega's control. He soon discovered, however, that Ruigi, the ruler of Kitagwenda, was not a supporter of Bunyoro, and so he changed his plan. Ruigi was to be left as chief but, a strange arrangement, subject to the suzerainty of Kasagama, and like the latter being obliged to carry out the Company's orders.[19] Two Sudanese garrisons were located in Kitagwenda to prevent any attack from Kabarega and to block the flow of arms and powder to Bunyoro, but in practice they proved a greater scourge to the country than the Mukama had ever done.

By these various stratagems Lugard hoped that he had brought a semblance of order to western Uganda, which was now sheltering behind a protective screen of stockades manned by Selim's Sudanese. He had laid the foundations of a reasonably orderly administration which appeared acceptable to the population as a whole because it was based on traditional principles. He had blocked Kabarega's supply routes, annexed the salt lake – the produce of which would be exchanged for limitless supplies of ivory, and he had prepared the ground for a further attack upon Bunyoro. He had also left one of his own officers, Captain Fenwick de Winton, to advise Kasagama.

Lugard thought that from the Company's point of view the expedition to the west must seem a great success, but almost at once his hopes received a severe setback. Scarcely had he set foot in Buganda once again than he received the news that for financial reasons the Company would have to withdraw from Uganda completely. Somehow, Lugard determined, he would hold on to Toro if to nothing else, and his associate in Buganda,

Captain Williams, offered his small private fortune to assist the enterprise. In the event the Company's proposal was not put into effect for almost a year, pending an investigation by the British Government of its own commitments in the area, but Lugard soon had his hands full as a result of a further outbreak of civil war in Buganda, and the west was left very much to its own devices.

With the dynamic presence of Lugard removed, Kasagama quickly showed signs of his own ambitions and of his strength of character. Emerging from the shadow of the older Yafeti he began to assume the status of ruler in his own right, which Lugard's policy had attempted to deny him. The presence of de Winton acted as something of a curb on his authority, but accompanying de Winton on a tour through the country from Fort Kivari to Fort Wavertree he was greeted happily by thousands of people who emerged from hiding now that the danger from Kabarega appeared at an end. He therefore took the opportunity to appoint chiefs in the regions through which he passed, thereby consolidating his own position vis-à-vis the people.[20] Among the triumphs of this expedition was the capture of Rwomire, who had handed over Kasagama's half-brothers to Kabarega nearly twenty years earlier, and de Winton wrote enthusiastically to Lugard about the achievements of both Kasagama and Yafeti.[21]

The strength of Toro's defences was tested at its northern and south-western extremities early in 1892 and proved to be sound. De Winton himself led a force to assist Karakwanzi in restoring his position in western Busongora after a raid by a rival chief. Simultaneously a strong army sent by Kabarega against Fort Wavertree was heavily defeated by the Sudanese garrison aided by a large force of Muhammadan Baganda under their leader, Mbogo, who hitherto had relied on Kabarega's aid in their struggle against Mwanga and the Christian Baganda.[22]

Kasagama himself had not been inactive, having joined de Winton in Kitagwenda before the latter was called away to

Busongora. Ruigi, the ruler of Kitagwenda, angered by the depredations of the Sudanese garrison, had left the district, and Kasagama, although succumbing temporarily to an attack of smallpox, sent an army under Nasanairi Mugurusi on a raid north-eastward into Kyaka district. This move was intended as no more than a sharp blow against Kabarega but it sounded a note of warning about Kasagama's intentions. Soon, too, he was left even more to his own devices. De Winton, who was attempting to negotiate for the continuing support of Mbogo and his Muhammadan Baganda with the prospect of their settling peacefully in the neighbourhood of their co-religionists, the Sudanese of the northern garrisons, died on 28 March 1892.[23] Fortunately for Toro, however, the Muhammadans moved away eastwards shortly afterwards and ceased to be a factor in the affairs of the kingdom.

Kasagama's authority was now challenged from another quarter. Yafeti Byakuyamba was envious of his protégé's success and began to make a bid for power, assisted by a group of Baganda who had accompanied him on his return with Lugard to Toro. Kasagama was convinced that Byakuyamba wished to divide Toro into two kingdoms, taking for himself the northern part bordering on Mwenge, of which he was a native. Fortune again favoured the young ruler. Byakuyamba's high-handed methods brought him swift retribution and he was taken prisoner by Sudanese troops from Fort Wavertree in response to an appeal from the Batoro of the Fort Portal region, who claimed they had been seriously ill-treated by his Baganda supporters. Kasagama was able to ransom his former guardian, but the Baganda remained unpopular. Byakuyamba therefore tried to promote his cause by visiting Buganda with his retinue, and while there he let it be known, albeit untruthfully, that Kasagama had abandoned Christianity and was worshipping pagan gods. A temporary reconciliation was achieved between the two former friends in the latter part of 1892 by the intervention of William Grant, with whom Byakuyamba returned to

Toro, but the trust which had previously marked their relationship steadily faded.

Kasagama's troubles did not end there. Early in 1893 Major Roderick Owen arrived with a proposal that Kasagama should abandon Toro and seek a new home in Kitagwenda because the Sudanese garrisons left by Lugard were to be withdrawn. This followed upon the I.B.E.A. Company's decision to pull out of Uganda and the recommendation of Sir Gerald Portal, who had been sent by the British Government to review the situation, that British protection should be limited to Buganda alone. After his efforts to assert his authority in Toro Kasagama was in no mood to retreat, and Owen sympathized with his plight although he had been made aware by the people of Busongora that Kasagama was not popular in that area. Owen also shared some of Lugard's views on the strategic and economic importance of western Uganda and so persuaded Portal to limit the withdrawal of Sudanese to the troops in the northern fort, Wavertree. At the same time he built another fort, named first Fort Jerry and later Fort Portal in honour of the British Commissioner, near to the site of Kasagama's new capital at Kabarole.

The presence of the Sudanese so close to Kasagama's headquarters was to prove a mixed blessing, because by raiding for food into Kabarega's territory as Lugard had encouraged them to do they fanned the flames of the Mukama's hatred for the breakaway kingdom. To add to Kasagama's difficulties, in June 1893 the Baganda Muhammadans began to negotiate with the Sudanese troops whom Lugard had taken into Buganda, and although the troops were disarmed before they could demonstrate any disloyalty to the British, fighting broke out between Protestant and Muslim Baganda in which the latter were defeated. Retreating westward they approached Toro and urged Kasagama to surrender to them. Fortunately the new threat was soon dispelled by the arrival of Baganda Christians, in pursuit of their opponents, but there followed an even more serious blow when, after Portal had returned to England in May, his successor as Commissioner, Captain J. R. L. Macdonald, decided to withdraw all the Sudanese forces from the west in fulfilment of his instructions to adopt a policy of retrenchment.

Kasagama's resilience was never more in evidence than during this testing period. In an attempt to solve a number of problems simultaneously he decided not to retreat but to advance. The Sudanese foraging expeditions had resulted in the withdrawal of the Banyoro *barasura* from Mwenge, Kitagweta, and even from Kyaka further to the east. Kasagama now determined to move into these regions, and at some stage in 1893, possibly as a follow-up to the discussions which had taken place with Grant, he appointed Byakuyamba Chief of Mwenge with the title of *Pokino*. Nyama, another Mubito who had been in exile in Buganda and who had accompanied him on his return to Toro in 1891, he made Chief of Kitagweta to the south of Mwenge, with the title of *Kitunzi*.

The appointment of Byakuyamba was a bold and also a hazardous move. In one sense the change of office might have been interpreted as demotion since he had formerly occupied a role very similar to that of *katikkiro*, or first minister, and in practice had exercised more influence than most *kitikkiros* might be expected to do. Now he was to have only the title of county chief which he might have been expected to resent. It was to Kasagama's advantage that Byakuyamba should be removed from the centre of affairs in Toro and at the same time he might well render conspicuous service to the kingdom by bringing new territory under its influence. On the other hand, Byakuyamba, as a native of Mwenge, was accepted by the Banyamwenge as their chief, if not with enthusiasm at least with tacit approval. Mugarra, the chief appointed by Kabarega, had been neither a Mubito nor a native of the district. Byakuyamba at once began to put his imprint on the county, appointing his own sub-chiefs and acting very much as an independent ruler. A devout Christian since his days in Buganda when he had come under the influence of the Church Missionary Society, he also built a church at his headquarters at Butiti.

Kasagama, meanwhile, sent an army into Bwamba in an attempt to establish his authority in that area also, while he stationed small patrols under the command of two of his trusted supporters, Mbogo on the borders of Mwenge, and Kasami, who was later to become chief of Bwamba, near Fort Wavertree. He himself prepared to go south to Katwe in an attempt to bring Busongora under his control.

There was little time to see how well these arrangements would work. Late in 1893 Kabarega sensed that his opportunity had come with the withdrawal of the Sudanese garrisons. He therefore launched an army against Mwenge under the command of one of his most successful generals, Rwabudongo. Kasagama, warned by Mbogo, hastened to intercept the invaders but Byakuyamba was defeated and had to withdraw southward. After pillaging Butiti and burning the church there, however, Rwabudongo withdrew and Byakuyamba was able to return and to take office once more. Kabarega, meanwhile, had turned his attention to Toro itself, when a Banyoro army had penetrated through the gap left by the withdrawal of the Fort Wavertree Sudanese garrison. Scattering Kasagama's army, the invaders advanced southward to burn his headquarters at Kabarole. Although the Batoro put up sporadic resistance Kasagama himself was forced to become a fugitive, avoiding capture by the narrowest of margins. He took refuge high on the Ruwenzori Mountains where many of his followers died of cold. Even there, however, he was not safe. Retreating to the north-west he sought the security of the Bwamba forest, but still the pursuit continued, until he eventually fled still further north towards the Semliki. Meanwhile Kabarega's main army ranged through Toro and into Busongora as far as Katwe, bringing retribution to all those who were not swift enough to fly beyond their reach.

After two months of living as a fugitive respite came to Kasagama, and once again it was due to the intervention of the British. Macdonald had at last come to the conclusion that the power of Bunyoro must be destroyed if the peace of the Lake Region was to be secured. Colonel H. E. Colvile, who arrived towards the end of 1893 to become Commissioner, agreed with him, seeing the removal of the threat from Bunyoro as a step to protect British interests in the Nile Valley. In January 1894, therefore, Colvile and Macdonald, with their small corps of troops and a large army of Baganda, marched against Bunyoro. The *barasura* in Toro were at once recalled to give Kabarega assistance and on the news of their departure Kasagama made his way, through the forest at first and then more boldly, to Katwe. The reception he was given was very different from that he had experienced a year earlier. Chastened by the ravages of the Banyoro, the Basongora welcomed the young man warmly. Shortly afterwards, too, came tidings of Kabarega's defeat, and Kasagama marched northward to Kabarole to re-establish his capital, arriving there in time to meet Major Owen who had been sent by Colvile to restore him as ruler in Toro.

The exchanges which then took place between the two reflect the confusion which existed about the disposition of authority. First, Owen consulted Kasagama regarding the boundaries of Toro and Kasagama made a generous estimate which owed more to his ambition than to historical accuracy. Owen, however, took him at his word, but somewhat surprisingly reported, 'I have reinstated Kasagama as King of Toro, Usongora and Kitakwenda, Yakyamba as Chief of Mwengi, and Kagisyri as Chief of Chatka, subject to Kasagama', and went on to specify the boundaries of the regions thus defined.[24] The treaty signed by Kasagama at Owen's request on 3 March 1894 was a printed form of the kind normally used by British agents in establishing a protectorate in Eastern Africa. It promised peace between Kasagama's subjects and those of the Queen of England and that the former would not cede territory to any Power or enter into any agreement with a foreign government except with the approval of the British Government. Gone was the British claim to sovereignty as set out in Lugard's agreement. Nevertheless, Owen saw fit to attach a statement that all the salt of Lake Katwe was claimed by the British, while Kasagama was required to pay a tax of 40 *frasilas* (34–36 lbs) of ivory a year, equal in value to £800. These stipulations clearly went beyond the powers implied by the expression 'protectorate' as interpreted by W. E. Hall in his *A Treatise on the Foreign Powers and Jurisdiction of the Crown*, published in the same year.[25] But they were consistent with the view of local practitioners – even those as sympathetic to African rulers as Owen was to Kasagama – who believed themselves entitled to assume whatever powers they thought necessary in an uncivilized country.[26]

Kasagama not unnaturally saw things in a different light. While recognizing that Kabarega's withdrawal was due to pressure from outside, he did not consider that he was in any other way beholden to Owen for his return to office. In his *Memoir* he states that he did not really understand Owen's treaty because he could neither read nor write, and there is no reason to disbelieve him. In any case, Owen had asked him to specify the limits of his kingdom and had accepted his definition, and neither Lugard nor Owen had been directly responsible for the extension of his influence in Busongora, Mwenge, Kitagweta and Kyaka, even though expansion into those districts had resulted indirectly from the activities of the Sudanese troops. At this stage Kasagama could only have assumed that Owen's treaty, far from being restrictive, indicated Britain's willingness to recognize the extension of his authority over an area at least twice as wide as that over which Kaboyo had ruled in his heyday. Byakuyamba, on the other hand, must have regarded his subservience to Kasagama, referred to in the treaty, as unmerited, since the latter had not helped in the recovery of Mwenge when it was overrun by Banyoro. Owen, meanwhile, unaware of these conflicting interpretations of his efforts, was simply attempting to impose a pattern which suited his concept of British interests, although the British Government itself was sceptical of the value of what he was doing.

The new relationships were soon tested when J. P. Wilson was sent to represent Britain in Toro. Wilson's first impressions of the kingdom and its inhabitants were unfavourable, for soon after crossing the border from Nkore he came upon people buying and selling women. Enquiring who had given permission for such dealings he was told that Yoswa Rusoke, whom Kasagama had made his *katikkiro*, together with the *Mujasi*, commander of Kasagama's armies, and a third person, Kamondo, had sanctioned the deal. Marching on to Kabarole, Wilson strode uninvited through the main gate and across the royal enclosure and made his camp alongside it. Kasagama was deeply angered by this discourtesy and was disturbed even more when Wilson went on to order the *katikkiro*, the *Mujasi* and Kamondo to be sent to him and on their arrival placed them in custody. Kasagama's mother paid a tusk of ivory to ransom the *katikkiro* and when Wilson left Kabarole, taking with him the other two prisoners, Kasagama himself hastened in pursuit and ransomed his *Mujasi* and Kamondo also.

This brush with the British must have given Kasagama cause for reflection, but he was a man who preferred action to recrimination and an opportunity for action occurred almost at once. He received a message from Byakuyamba saying that Rwabudongo, the Munyoro general, had attacked Mwenge. Kasagama responded quickly by sending an army commanded by Yoswa Rusoke to Byakuyamba's aid, but by the time help arrived the Banyoro had withdrawn. Kasagama therefore determined to make his own mark and at the same time to rid his country of the constant danger of attack. With his characteristic lack of rancour he asked Wilson for troops to assist him in a campaign to Bunyoro. Wilson refused, but Kasagama was not deflected from his enterprise. With his own levies he crossed the

Muzizi River and in cooperation with Byakuyamba and the Chiefs of Kyaka and Kitagweta led a foray into Buyaga and even sent an expedition into the Bugoma Forest. The sequel to the campaign suggested that Kasagama was becoming a force in his own right, for Rwabudongo offered to surrender. Kasagama sent Rusoke to bring in the Munyoro commander and himself acted as intermediary between Wilson and Rwabudongo when the latter made his submission.

Kasagama's uneven progress unfortunately still continued. Wilson was recalled to Kampala in June 1895 and was replaced by Captain Ashburnham, a man whose view of Britain's relations with Toro was even more authoritarian than that of his predecessor. He appears to have taken an immediate dislike to Kasagama, believing him guilty of robbing Rwabudongo of rifles and clothing. Putting the young ruler in chains he beat the *katikkiro* and the treasurer until they told him where Kasagama kept his stock of ivory. He then seized twenty tusks, along with cattle and goats belonging to Kasagama, and although the latter was then set free Ashburnham remained suspicious of him, listening readily to the charges brought against the young man by local inhabitants who held a grudge or who hoped for plunder at their ruler's expense. A message to the effect that Kasagama was obtaining cartridges illegally from Baziba traders led to a raid on the township of Kabarole by Sudanese troops, although when Kasagama demanded an explanation Ashburnham disclaimed all knowledge of what had taken place. Nevertheless, on the following day, 14 November 1895, Ashburnham ordered Kasagama's arrest. But Kasagama fled to the mountains and was later able to take advantage of Ashburnham's preoccupation elsewhere to escape to Buganda where he protested to the Commissioner, Ernest Berkeley, about his treatment.

While in Buganda Kasagama took a step which was to have an important effect upon his subsequent career. In 1894 the Church Missionary Society had sent Baganda teachers to Toro and although their arrival did not deeply affect Kasagama he received them in a friendly manner. Now, in his time of trial, he received teaching from the missionaries and was baptized in Namirembe Cathedral on 15 March 1896. The previous month the Commissioner had decided that Ashburnham had acted wrongly towards Kasagama, and in addition to granting compensation he also agreed that the ivory tax should be greatly reduced and that the young ruler was to be allowed to take two-thirds of any salt produced at Katwe. Ashburnham was recalled shortly afterwards and replaced by Captain Sitwell who was given instructions to soft-pedal British interference.[27] Kasagama therefore returned to Toro with considerable satisfaction, to be followed shortly afterwards on 3 April 1896 by Bishop Tucker and the Rev. A. B. Fisher, who was to reside at Kabarole and become a staunch supporter of the young ruler. The missionaries subsequently gave Kasagama loyal aid, partly because they believed they were right to do so and partly because they were convinced that a Protestant monarch would greatly assist the work of the mission in Toro, a view which was strengthened when Kasagama was confirmed on 10 May 1896, two days after the baptism of his wife and mother.

The missionaries' support proved a mixed blessing to Kasagama, however. Fisher had been preceded to Toro by Père Achte of the rival White Fathers' Mission and Sitwell criticized the ruler for showing favouritism to the adherents of the Protestant Mission at the expense of the followers of the White Fathers. His intervention marked an interesting stage in the development of Britain's relations with Toro. In the course of 1896 British protection was extended over Toro and other parts of western Uganda simply by means of a pronouncement made in Britain and without any local negotiations or any further definition of Britain's role in the area.[28] So far as Kasagama was concerned, even if he knew of this new development his relations with Britain must have seemed unchanged. Sitwell, however, disturbed by the young man's continuing intolerance towards Roman Catholics, toyed with the idea of replacing him as ruler by his brother, who had recently returned from exile in Bunyoro. Sitwell's interpretation of the role of the protecting state thus implied the right to determine who should rule the protected state, but he appears to have accepted the fact that some residual authority rested in the ruling dynasty.

Stephen Bagge, who replaced Sitwell in March 1899, adopted a different attitude, doing everything possible to build up the morale and status of the Mukama. Kasagama himself recorded that Bagge consistently maintained that whoever rebelled against him must be punished, and when chiefs complained that Kasagama had reduced their jurisdiction Bagge merely replied that this was a field in which the Mukama had complete authority, and discouraged people from informing secretly against their ruler. In these various ways the status of the Mukama was raised from the lowly position to which it had sunk under Ashburnham when it was widely recognized that the young ruler was out of favour with the British.[29]

During the later 1890s, when British influence in Toro was exercised only lightly and when the Church Missionary Society was doing all in its power to enhance his status, Kasagama was able to take great strides towards imposing his personal authority throughout the kingdom. Busongora, which had so long held out against his overlordship, accepted his rule with some alacrity as an alternative to the ravages of Kabarega. Mwenge, however, presented more difficult problems. There Byakuyamba still rankled under Kasagama's suzerainty and was determined to establish himself as Mukama of eastern Toro. First, therefore, he made a bid to extend his authority southward and eastward over Kitagweta and Kyaka in the hope of strengthening his claim to recognition as an independent ruler. The young chief of Kitagweta, Nyama, appealed to Kasagama and the British to protect his interests and Byakuyamba's scheme was frustrated. Subsequently he became involved in the rising of Kabaka Mwanga of Buganda against the British in 1897 and then committed suicide. Kasagama was thus left in undisputed control of Mwenge and placed his own nominee in charge.

The Mukama then turned his attention to Kitagwenda where he encountered more prolonged opposition, for Kitagwenda had a history of several generations of near autonomy under the suzerainty of Bunyoro. Ruigi, the chief whom Lugard had arbitrarily placed under Kasagama's suzerainty in 1891, left the country shortly afterwards for Bunyoro where he died of smallpox. Kitagwenda was then administered by his brother Kakintule, on behalf of Ruigi's young son, Bulemu. Kakintule adopted a consistently independent attitude towards Kasagama because he regarded Toro as a kingdom of only recent origin, and at times he had dealings with Kabarega and with Mugabe Ntare of Nkore. Early in 1898 both Mwanga of Buganda and Ntare's successor in Nkore, Kahaya, took refuge in Kitagwenda to escape the turmoil which had arisen in Buganda as a result of Mwanga's attempt to break with British domination. Thinking less of Kitagwenda's relationship with Toro than of the need to deal with Mwanga, Captain Sitwell set out for Kitagwenda in January 1898 with a Sudanese force and accompanied by Nasanairi Mugurusi, Chief of Mwenge and shortly to be *katikkiro*. Kasagama followed shortly afterwards with nearly 3000 armed men and Mwanga was forced to withdraw.

Kakintule, meanwhile, had had dealings with the White Fathers' Mission and, although he had finally decided to oppose the admission of catechists to his country, he was skilful enough to use his negotiations with the French missionaries to enhance his own authority. In 1898, however, he committed a serious blunder. After some minor dispute he ordered the massacre of a party of Batoro who were passing through his country. Kasagama took prompt action and sent an army commanded by Yoswa Rusoke to Kitagwenda. Kakintule fled and the young Bulemu was appointed by Kasagama to a junior chieftainship in his own country. On the complaint of the Mukama, however, he was shortly afterwards sent to Entebbe, and Kasagama then seized the opportunity to introduce chiefs of his own selection at all levels throughout the country.[30] Sir Harry Johnston, who at the time was Special Commissioner in Uganda, kept Bulemu in Entebbe for a few months and then sent him back to Toro with instructions that Kasagama should teach him the duties of a chief in preparation for reinstatement at a later date.[31] Questions were asked about his religion and the Rev. A. B. Fisher, a particularly volatile missionary, came to blows with a member of the White Fathers' Mission in defence of his claim to the young chief's allegiance.[32] Bulemu himself was then consulted and stated that he was a Protestant, not, it would seem, in enthusiastic response to Fisher's display of muscular Christianity, but because Kasagama had insisted that this should be his answer. The Mukama was already learning the value of religious solidarity as a cement to political power.

As the century closed, Kasagama, by force and by guile if not with universal acclaim, was establishing himself firmly as ruler of a greatly enlarged Toro which included Busongora, Mwenge, Kyaka, Kitagweta and Kitagwenda as well as the heartland of Toro proper. To his disappointment the British did not permit him to include the territory to the south of the Kazinga Channel in his kingdom, the plain and the hilly country of Bunyaruguru beyond being incorporated within the enlarged domain of the Mugabe of Ankole. Although it was necessary in 1898 and 1899 to send small military expeditions into various districts to subdue either internal or external threats to his authority Kasagama's nominees, Protestants for the greater part, were occupying the important offices both at the centre and in the provinces, and when chiefs Sinasi Kagoro and Kagwahabi protested at their demotion by Kasagama, Bagge insisted that the matter was for the Mukama alone to determine. Many important appointments and transfers were in fact taking place, including the elevation of Nasanairi Mugurusi to the office of *katikkiro* at the instance of Stephen Bagge, who considered Yoswa Rusoke an admirable soldier but unsuited to the more sophisticated demands now imposed upon the Mukama's chief adviser. It was in recognition of the growing complexity of the kingdom's administration also that a number of the more important *saza* (county) chiefs were given assistants, all of them nominated by Kasagama.

The happy interaction between the Mukama and the representative of the Protectorate Administration provided reassurance and guaranteed a minimum of British intervention in Toro's affairs. Meanwhile the agents of the Church Missionary Society solidly supported the concept of monarchical authority inherent in Kasagama's outlook, happy in the knowledge that their work was flourishing under his benign patronage. The Roman Catholic missionaries were less satisfied with the situation, claiming on a number of occasions that county chiefs, and even the *katikkiro*, treated their supporters unfairly. The Mukama, they said, took no steps to curb these injustices. In his typically forthright manner Kasagama called on Père Roche and asked him to supply examples of the ill-treatment of which he complained, but according to the Mukama himself the missionary failed to respond.[33] However, Kasagama was summoned to Entebbe in 1899 to explain what was taking place, after which there was an improvement in his treatment of Catholics.

The land question provides an interesting example of the manner in which the complicated interplay of authority between the British agents and Kasagama unconsciously reinforced the latter's confidence in his ultimate sovereignty. In 1899 the British Prime Minister, the Marquis of Salisbury, proposed that Colonel Trevor Ternan, Acting Commissioner in Uganda, should issue regulations forbidding the transfer of native land to any foreigner without the approval of the British representative in the district concerned.[34] This information was transmitted to Kasagama by Bagge with the further elaboration that the ban on land purchase in Toro applied equally to

Baganda and Basongora because the country belonged to the Batoro alone. The news confirmed Kasagama's own appraisal of the situation and although at this stage the young ruler was happy to work in association with Bagge, and even to accept Bagge's word as contributing additional authority to his own opinion, as time went on he assumed the right to distribute the land as he saw fit, in the manner of the *Bakama* of Bunyoro in former times.

So the Kingdom of Toro was restored, and because its ruler adopted the panoply of power of his Banyoro forefathers the new kingdom acquired an aura of antiquity and the authority conveyed by traditions which were, perhaps, appropriate to its rulers if not to the kingdom itself. The British, meanwhile, looked on with satisfaction only occasionally tinged with doubt. The country had achieved comparative peace and orderliness with a minimum of expense, and it remained to be seen what profit Britain could derive from the situation.

IV · The Kingdom Confirmed

The next act in the establishment of the Kingdom of Toro and of its relations with Britain opened with the arrival in Uganda of Special Commissioner Sir Harry Johnston in December 1899. Johnston's commission granted him the title of Commander in Chief and Consul General, thus observing the niceties of the protectorate situation. But it also gave him a fairly free hand, provided he bore in mind the need for economy, to organize the administration of the Protectorate along the lines which he thought best.

Johnston's first efforts were directed towards making an agreement with Buganda, about which he had been given rather more specific instructions in view of the treaty of 1893 between Mwanga and the British. The Commission contained no similar reference to Owen's treaty of 1894 with Toro, so that in view of his general instructions to avoid all but minor alterations in Uganda Johnston seems to have intended only to reaffirm the *status quo* in the western kingdom with, possibly, some attempt at a clearer definition of the terms of the agreement with Britain.

Kasagama was watching warily, however, and his suspicions seemed justified by Johnston's manner on his arrival at Fort Portal in June 1900. In spite of the warm welcome the Commissioner received and his clumsy flattery of the Batoro in his opening address[1] his subsequent behaviour was brusque and dictatorial. Mr H. E. Maddox of the Church Missionary Society, who was present on the occasion, wrote later that Johnston summoned the Batoro together and then orally rendered into Swahili a document, typed in English, which was then translated by an African interpreter into Luganda which only some

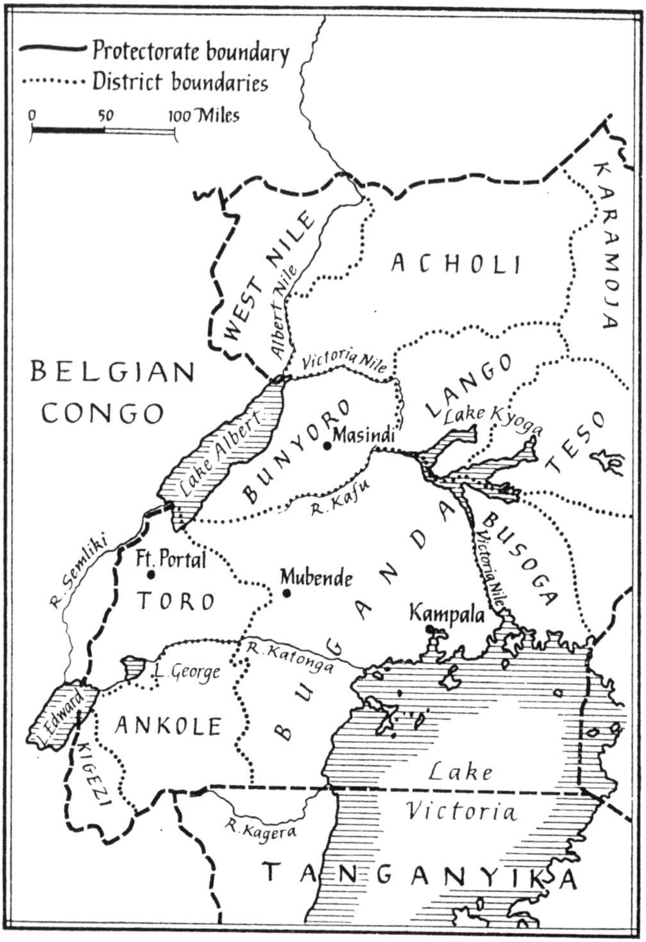

Part of the Uganda Protectorate

of the leading chiefs understood. No questions or discussions were allowed and the Mukama and chiefs, although asking for time to translate the document, were required to sign an agreement of which they scarcely understood the contents, on pain of losing their chieftainship if they refused.

Under the terms of the Agreement the boundaries of the Kingdom of Toro were defined for the first time and in addition to Toro Proper embraced the *sazas* of Mwenge, Kitagwenda, Kitagweta, Kyaka and Nyakabimba. Bwamba was included within these limits but was to be administered by the representative of the Protectorate Administration stationed in Toro until agreement had been reached on the boundary between Uganda and the Congo Free State. In the remainder of the district Kasagama was to have a dual role. He was to be personally responsible for the administration of what was now designated Toro Proper, which included Busongora, and at the same time he would be *supreme* chief over the whole district although there would be *saza* chiefs in charge of each of the five counties outside Toro Proper. This double function was further emphasized by the grant to Kasagama of the right to receive ten per cent of the taxes collected throughout the whole district, as well as a further ten per cent from Toro Proper, while the *saza* chiefs were permitted to receive only ten per cent of the taxes collected in their own counties. Grants of land were also made to the Mukama and to each of the *saza* chiefs in their official capacity as well as further grants of private land which could be handed on to their heirs. Again, Kasagama was entitled to hold private land in all the *sazas* although his official land must be taken from Toro Proper. Thereafter, all land which at the time of the signing of the Agreement was waste or uncultivated, together with all minerals and salt deposits, was to become the property of the British Government.

The two other main provisions concerned taxation and the administration of justice. Hut and gun taxes were to be paid by all adult males in the district and henceforward no chiefs would be entitled to levy tribute of any kind. Justice between natives of Toro was to be administered in the first instance by the *saza* chiefs though there was a right of appeal in important cases to a supreme court which the British, using the Luganda expression, referred to as the *lukiiko*, but which the Batoro preferred to call the *Rukurato*. The composition of this body was not laid down but traditionally it consisted of the leading chiefs to whom the Mukama looked for advice. Ultimately an appeal might be laid before the European official if the case involved a heavy penalty. Finally, it was stated that in the event of either the Mukama or any other of the signatories breaking the Agreement they might be deposed and the Agreement annulled, leaving the Protectorate Administration free to substitute any other method of local government in Toro.

Later in the day and with Johnston's consent Kasagama took the Agreement to Maddox to have it translated, when it was immediately seen that the Commissioner had not fully grasped the situation in the kingdom. He had, in particular, overlooked the fact that Toro Proper had already been divided by Kasagama into a number of *sazas*, but no provision had been made for the *saza* chiefs. When approached about this matter Johnston was not prepared to revise the administrative subdivision of Toro but he did agree to an addendum which granted private land to eight chiefs named by Kasagama, though they were not to receive any official land.[2]

Johnston's behaviour throughout the negotiations might give the impression that the declaration of a protectorate had given Britain full authority to determine the constitution of Toro. Sir William Gowers, when Governor of Uganda a quarter of a century later, held the view that the Agreement was no more than a solemn declaration of policy by the protecting power which, having driven out the Banyoro and re-established the Toro kingdom, was free to dispose of the kingdom as it thought fit.[3] It seems clear, however, that Johnston had aimed solely at creating an atmosphere of greater stability in Toro, and

Kasagama himself appears to have accepted the Agreement as an acknowledgement of his own rightful authority, while his subsequent criticisms were directed against those arrangements which he believed to have been the results of honest errors in Johnston's interpretation of the traditional situation in Toro. The definition of the boundaries of the kingdom, innovation though it was, was looked upon by the Mukama not as a restriction but as a welcome recognition of Toro's existence in its new form and an incentive to him to expand his authority to fill the whole region adequately.

In other respects, however, the Agreement had already been overtaken by events. As Kasagama pointed out, *saza* chiefs had never previously possessed the right to nominate their successors, a function which had always been performed by the Mukama. He himself had appointed Byakuyamba and his successors as chiefs of Mwenge, and Nyama as chief of Kitagweta, while even in Kitagwenda, where the chieftainship had been hereditary for some generations, he had already ousted Bulemu once and was to do so again. He had, too, already exercised the traditional right of a Mukama of Bunyoro to allocate estates to his supporters even in the *sazas* now declared by the Agreement to be administered by other chiefs, and he had certainly done so without the consent of those chiefs. This was a right essential to the authority of a ruler because he had no other means of rewarding his supporters or of paying minor chiefs for fulfilling essential duties. Furthermore, to prevent the chiefs levying tribute from the inhabitants of land which they had been granted was not only to restrict their rightful income but would seriously undermine their authority. For the Protectorate Administration to claim the income from the salt trade was also a serious blow to Kasagama. Although he was later permitted to lease the deposits in return for the payment of rent to the Protectorate authorities, he remained resentful because the Protectorate Administration retained the right to withdraw the lease if it saw fit to do so.

In practice, the Agreement might have seriously restricted Kasagama's sovereignty if it had been fully observed, for it contained the tacit assumption that ultimate authority now lay in the hands of Britain. Kasagama was no longer the supreme source of justice since an appeal could be made to the Protectorate's representative in serious cases; the land was not wholly at his disposal; he was no longer entitled to levy tribute, and he had no control over the appointment of his more senior chiefs. There were, however, as the Mukama quickly appreciated, loopholes which might be exploited by a man of initiative, and he at once renewed the constitutional struggle on three fronts. If the Agreement challenged his interpretation of the traditional role of the Toro monarchy then he must circumvent it. It would be necessary to clarify his relations with the Protectorate Administration; he must demonstrate his complete authority over the *saza* chiefs; and he must assert the identity of Toro vis-à-vis the neighbouring kingdoms.

It was in his relations with his neighbours that Kasagama's position was most quickly put to the test. In August 1900 George Wilson was appointed Sub-Commissioner for the Western Province, which was deemed to include the three kingdoms of Bunyoro, Toro and the enlarged kingdom of Ankole, formerly Nkore. In October Wilson wrote to the collectors, as the Protectorate agents were significantly called, in Toro and Ankole, remarking that in his opinion there was a tendency for the Protectorate authorities to regard the various districts as virtually separate countries instead of being integral parts of the whole territory. Believing Toro and Bunyoro to be closely allied in traditions and sympathies, he proposed as a preliminary step to ask the collector of Toro to bring Kasagama and a number of his chiefs to meet the young ruler of Bunyoro. His aim was to establish a general council of chiefs of the Western Province in order to formulate a common policy for their domestic administration. Wilson understood the people he was dealing with as fully as any British official ever did, and he was not unaware of the rulers' reluctance to surrender their independence. He foresaw Kasagama's distrust of his proposal but believed his aim to be sufficiently important to persevere with it.[4]

The meeting took place in April 1901, and the Rev. A. B. Fisher described it, at least from his own point of view, as a successful encounter. Kasagama and his chiefs, he said, took the opportunity to testify to the benefits of Christianity in the presence of the young ruler and his advisers.[5] Wilson's account was less favourable. According to him, Kasagama and his chiefs insulted Byabachwezi, one of the leading chiefs of Bunyoro, and subsequently the Mukama refused to acknowledge any communication from the ruler of Bunyoro or to enter into any correspondence with him.

While Kasagama's hauteur on this occasion may be explained in part by his anxiety to avoid any suggestion of Toro's subordination to Bunyoro, it was of a part with his attitude towards his other neighbours and sprang from his desire to assert Toro's independence, which Wilson appeared intent upon destroying. The same attitude was evident in Kasagama's relations with Ankole. The Mukama was resentful at the inclusion of the territory to the south of the Kazinga Channel and to the south-east of Lake George within the neighbouring kingdom and his anger was reflected in his petulant behaviour over a number of trading transactions with Ankole. He displayed a corresponding arrogance in 1902 or 1903 when he threatened to sue one of the Baganda regents, Zacharia Kisingiri, for the value of several tusks of ivory lost in transit in 1898 when Kisingiri had acted as consignee purely out of courtesy. Again in 1904, Nasanairi Mugurusi, the *katikkiro* of Toro, delivered an address on Kasagama's behalf to the Buganda *Lukiiko* which that body regarded as wholly insolent.[6] The Mukama, however, believed that he must defend his position whenever a dispute arose, and he was not, in fact, the only aggressor. Due to a lack of accuracy in the definition of boundaries in the Buganda and Toro Agreements of 1900, differences of opinion arose in 1903 over the location of the frontier between the two kingdoms. With all danger from Kabarega removed, the Baganda had been expanding westward into the Kyaka district claimed by Toro.[7]

Kasagama took equally prompt action to ensure that his authority over the chiefs in the outlying districts of his own kingdom should not suffer as a result of the Agreement. In 1900 he granted land to his supporters – including the *katikkiro*, Nasanairi Mugurusi – in the counties of Kitagwenda, Mwenge and Kyaka without consulting, and indeed against the wishes of, the *saza* chiefs of those areas, and in some cases after evicting the original occupiers. In Mwenge and Kyaka he also appointed minor chiefs, again without seeking the approval of the *saza* chiefs concerned.[8] In both these instances he was acting as any Mukama of Bunyoro would have done, and it was this role which he pursued persistently. The British official, R. Baile, who was in Toro at the time, was himself anxious to strengthen Kasagama's position in order to secure peaceful administration in the district, and his successors, although convinced that the Mukama was contravening the spirit of the Agreement by interfering in such a high-handed fashion in counties which were only under his suzerainty, were reluctant to disturb a *fait accompli*. The inhabitants of the areas concerned, none of whom could formerly have regarded themselves as Batoro or subjects of Kasagama, could only accept their lot, although they may well have resented their subjugation to an upstart ruler. Once again, by his prompt action Kasagama had undermined the force of the Agreement.

In Kitagwenda he was less successful, although in 1903 he resisted pressure from Protectorate officials to restore Bulemu, the hereditary chief of the district.[9] Instead he installed his father-in-law, Nicodemu Kakurora, and managed to control a resentful population with the aid of a small but active police force.[10] On 9 February 1903, however, the Mukama could hold out no longer and Bulemu was appointed chief of Kitagwenda by the Commissioner at a *baraza* (assembly) held in Fort Portal.[11] Even then, however, Kasagama did not give in entirely. He asked that the *katikkiro* should be permitted to accompany the collector, Mr F. Ormsby, when he went to reinstate Bulemu, so that the people should see that the collector was acting in concert with the Toro Government and not independently of it.[12] The people of Kitagwenda nevertheless remained hostile to Kasagama's rule and in 1911 the *mumyuka*, a senior chief named Danieri Kakete, crossed into Ankole, taking with him a hundred of his followers.

The district boundaries imposed by the Protectorate Administration were not, it is true, regarded very seriously by many of the inhabitants of Uganda. Pastoralists in particular ignored artificial administrative frontiers which interfered with their seasonal search for grazing grounds for their cattle. But this move by the Bagwenda was not simply a protest against irksome restrictions. It resembled more nearly the feudal act of diffidation. The *mumyuka* wished to demonstrate that he no longer accepted Kasagama as his overlord and instead was offering himself and his people as subjects of the Mugabe of Ankole. Protectorate officials tried to persuade Kakete to return to Kitagwenda because his action threatened the orderly administrative pattern they were attempting to substitute for the dynamic political life which had formerly existed in western Uganda and which they preferred to regard as merely chaotic.[13]

In Kitagweta Kasagama was more successful. He had originally appointed Nyama, at that time a pliant youth, as *saza* chief, and when the young man was found guilty of misappropriating hut tax and had to be deposed the Mukama quickly replaced him by another of his own nominees, Kalyegira. The latter, however, claimed that by virtue of the Agreement he was a semi-autonomous ruler, owing allegiance to the Protectorate authorities rather than to Kasagama. The acting-collector, Mr J. A. Haldane, was more sympathetic to the Mukama's problems than Ormsby – who had criticized Kasagama for his consistently irritating behaviour towards every county chief outside Toro Proper. Although he had considerable sympathy for the *saza* chiefs, having in the course of his tour of Toro heard a number of complaints against the Mukama, Haldane twice intervened early in 1905 in an attempt to persuade Kalyegira to accept his subordination to Kasagama with good grace. He was not unaware of the terms of the Agreement and he had no intention of increasing Kasagama's authority or of attempting to unify the country under him, but he did wish to avoid the petty clashes which encouraged the Mukama to use his power for personal ends.[14]

What Haldane did not fully appreciate was that Kasagama did not consider that he was acting pettily or for purely personal gain. Every action was part of his scheme to enhance the role of the monarchy, and although he himself enjoyed the exercise of power his efforts transcended personal ambition. He was simply recreating within the boundaries generously recognized by the Protectorate Administration a state which matched in its organization, if not in its extent, the former Empire of Bunyoro-Kitara. This meant that the Mukama was the source of all authority and *saza* chiefs were simply his agents. So, despite the Agreement, the chiefs of Toro were moved round from one county to another in rapid succession and not one of them was given the opportunity to choose his heir. That was the prerogative of the Mukama.

Westward, towards the Congo, Kasagama's efforts were frustrated in spite of the help he derived from members of the Church Missionary Society, who were intent upon extending their own influence and recognized the benefits which might accrue to them from cooperating with the Mukama. Officially excluded from Bwamba by the Agreement, Kasagama became restless when he saw the British did not themselves show any signs of urgent action, for there appeared a lively possibility that the Belgians might seize the opportunity to occupy land to which he himself laid claim. Even the Katwe Salt Lake was not safe. In 1897 Manyema soldiers who had rebelled against their Belgian commander had attacked Fort George but had been repulsed by the garrison left there by the British.[15] Moreover, the Belgian authorities themselves appeared to condone if not actually to instigate frequent raids across the Semliki River into country of which the ownership was still in dispute. Although the situation caused both worry and inconvenience for the Protectorate officials they continued to exercise restraint. Bagge, acting Sub-Commissioner of the Western Province, drew the Commissioner's attention in 1902 to the difficulties to which the undemarcated boundary gave rise and mentioned that in 1896 Captain Sitwell had advocated that the Semliki River should be made the boundary between Uganda and the Congo Free State so that the dividing line would be easily recognizable.[16] As late as 1905, however, Colonel Hayes Sadler was still urging the Colonial Office to seek the cooperation of King Leopold II in putting an end to demands for salt from Lake Katwe by the Belgians, pending the delimitation of the boundary between the two countries.[17]

The C.M.S. missionaries were as irked by the Administration's inaction as was Kasagama himself. To them the limitless territory to the west cried out for attention. As early as 1900 the C.M.S. had established a mission in Bwamba and had also extended their activities across the River Semliki into Mboga.[18] Their work in the latter district was greatly assisted by the presence of Chief Paulo Rabolo, who was in charge of the whole area; he was himself a Christian, and in 1901 the first five converts were baptized.[19] In spite of the fact that Sir Harry Johnston had insisted that Mboga should remain independent of Toro the missionaries from Fort Portal managed to maintain regular contact and even cast hopeful glances still further westward. As the Rev. T. B. Johnson pointed out in 1903, much of the territory claimed by the Congo Free State lay within a week's journey from Fort Portal, or only half that time from Mboga, while the nearest Free State mission was at Stanleyville, a month's journey distant. The survey carried out in 1901 for the proposed Cape to Cairo Railway had also introduced an element of urgency into the campaign to evangelize the people of that region, lest the arrival of the railway should make it more difficult to spread the Gospel[20] by introducing the oppressive system of forced labour for which the Congo Free State was already becoming notorious.

Kasagama would gladly have supported the missionaries' efforts but the Protectorate authorities restrained him. Although contact was made with the people of Mboga[21] and Bwamba,[22] the Mukama's desire to appoint a chief in that county after the inhabitants had been harassed by the Belgians was firmly discouraged by the collector.[23] Kasagama persisted, however, and eventually, when he had to find an appointment for his father-in-law, Nicodemu, after the latter's dismissal from Kitagwenda in 1903, the Mukama sought to post him to Bwamba. Nicodemu had little stomach for this dangerous assignment and, having demonstrated that he was afraid to live among the Baamba, left his son-in-law with no option but to restrain his enthusiasm for the time being. With the Governor's approval, however, Kasagama was able to leave an acting chief in Bwamba on the clear understanding that he would interfere as little as possible with the people, and this was an arrangement with which the chief could easily comply because the Baamba took no heed of him.[24]

The Anglo-Congolese Boundary Agreement of 10 May 1910 was a bitter disappointment to Kasagama. Not only was he forced to surrender all claim to Mboga, but, although Bwamba now reverted to Toro, the Protectorate authorities decided that the Batoro chiefs had been so ineffective that the most satisfactory arrangement for the future would be for the chiefs to receive fixed salaries, paid by the Protectorate Administration, and to remain under the supervision of Protectorate officials rather than of the Mukama's Government, until the condition of the district had improved. Resilient as ever, Kasagama attempted to obtain compensation for these setbacks by asking for the transfer from Ankole of land to which he laid claim on the basis of ancient authority, but again he was disappointed.[25] Even as late as 1926, by which time Bwamba had for two years been administered as part of Toro District and was paying ten per cent of its income from poll tax into the kingdom's treasury to meet the salaries of the chiefs, Kasagama still did not feel he had a secure hold upon the county. Indeed, since 1920 all the land in Bwamba had been treated as the property of the Crown to protect the inhabitants from the depredations of Batoro landlords.

Kasagama's struggle to demonstrate his sovereignty over the outlying districts of the kingdom was paralleled by his efforts to clarify his position in what the Agreement had referred to as Toro Proper. In this latter area he was recognized as chief, but only it would seem as *saza* chief – which made him little more than a *primus inter pares* as far as the chiefs of Mwenge, Kitagwenda and the other *sazas* were concerned. In Toro Proper, however, the chiefs appointed by the Mukama had continued to carry out their duties in spite of being fined by the Protectorate officials if they were caught doing so. George Wilson was asked to investigate the problems cited by Kasagama in 1901 and was able to get the Commissioner's approval for the revival of the *saza* chieftainships in Toro Proper and for the payment of the *katikkiro* out of funds subscribed by those chiefs.[26] Colonel Sadler, the next Commissioner, was not amenable to Wilson's proposals and subsequently rescinded the arrangement Wilson had made because he believed it to be a breach of the 1900 Agreement. In 1903, and again in 1904, Sadler told Kasagama that the men he was sponsoring as *saza* chiefs had no claim to the title and went on to add somewhat gratuitously that even the real *saza* chiefs would not have been acknowledged by the Batoro if it had not been for British intervention.[27] He also rejected the *katikkiro's* appeal for payment from hut tax, arguing that he was an appointee of

Kasagama, and not of the Protectorate, and must therefore look to the Mukama for reimbursement for his services. Sadler was firmly of the opinion that Kasagama had been prompted by the would-be chiefs themselves to raise the issue, but this was almost certainly not the case. The Mukama had consistently included these men among the membership of his *Rukurato*, the composition of which had never been laid down by the Agreement, and he clearly relied upon their support in his efforts to assert his authority over the other *saza* chiefs. They, in turn, simply looked to him to restore them to what they believed to be their true position.

The *Rukurato* was effectively Kasagama's instrument, because it consisted of himself, the *katikkiro*, the eight '*saza*' chiefs of Toro Proper and the five *saza* chiefs mentioned in the Agreement. In 1903, however, the Sub-Commissioner for the Western Province, Mr J. P. Wilson, attempted to interpret the Agreement more accurately by amending the constitution of the *Rukurato*. Henceforward, Toro Proper was to be represented only by Kasagama and his *katikkiro*, while each of the other *sazas* would have one voting member.[28] If this plan had been put into effect it would have undermined the position of the Mukama irrevocably. Colonel Sadler, however, recommended that Toro Proper should have four members and, on Kasagama's insistence, agreed that the number should be increased to five.[29] While this arrangement only gave numerical parity to Toro Proper it helped to restore Kasagama's status as overlord, a role which the other chiefs of Toro Proper were happy to accord him because to do so helped to enhance their own position. An attempt in 1905 by the acting Sub-Commissioner Western Province, Harry Galt, to achieve official recognition of the role of the *katikkiro* by authorizing his payment from Protectorate funds was defeated by the Acting-Commissioner, Mr J. F. Cunningham, who referred Galt to Sadler's earlier ruling.[30]

Kasagama was tenacious. Later in the year he approached

George Wilson, inviting him to take up his case. Wilson considered that his involvement in the affairs of Toro in 1901 left him with an obligation to see the proposals he had then made put into effect. Quoting the evidence of Mr H. E. Maddox, who said that the Agreement had been drafted and introduced in a hasty and arbitrary fashion, he asked for a review of the position. Colonel Sadler was unsympathetic but, being near the end of his tour of duty, asked one of the Protectorate officials, Mr F. A. Knowles, to investigate the situation and to submit a report so that his successor could have the necessary information available before reaching a decision. The report was submitted when Sadler was on the verge of leaving Uganda and, pending the arrival of the new Commissioner, the matter was left to be dealt with by the Acting-Commissioner, who was none other than George Wilson.

Knowles' report was accompanied by a petition from the Toro *Rukurato* which contained five requests. It asked that Kasagama should cease to be *saza* chief of Toro and should be simply Mukama of the whole country; that Toro Proper should be divided into four *sazas*, later to be increased to five by the inclusion of Bwamba when the frontier was finally decided; that the *saza* chiefs thus restored should be entitled to appoint their heirs, subject to the approval of the *Rukurato*; that the question of land ownership be clarified; and that the Mukama be permitted to give his ten per cent of the income from Toro Proper in salaries to the four new *saza* chiefs while his income from the Capital, together with further sums to be paid by the *saza* chiefs, should be made available as a salary for the *katikkiro*. They were prepared to accept that three of the smaller *sazas* into which Kasagama had divided Toro Proper should be abolished, but asked that the chiefs of those counties should be permitted to retain for their lifetime the personal land granted to them under the addendum to the Agreement. A further request was made that the succession to the office of Mukama should be restricted to the descendants of Kaboyo and, looking with some concern at the neighbouring kingdom of Bunyoro where the troubled situation had led the Protectorate Administration to appoint Baganda agents, it was urged that, so long as the Agreement was honoured, only Batoro should be allowed to sit in the *Rukurato*.[31]

The terms of the petition made its origin abundantly clear. The five chiefs of the existing *sazas* added their signatures without any enthusiasm and under pressure from Kasagama. They were fully aware that by giving their support, however unwillingly, they were striking a blow at their own status by attempting to elevate four other chiefs to their own level and by placing themselves so completely under the Mukama's sovereignty. Wilson, however, was in no doubt that Knowles' report, which was sympathetic to Kasagama's aims, should be put into effect. The one issue which could not be settled was that of land because it was expected that a report on land tenure in the whole of the Western Province would soon be tabled and the Acting Commissioner was anxious not to pre-judge the situation. The other recommendations were accepted by the Colonial Secretary, Lord Elgin, who commended them to the new Commissioner, Sir Hesketh Bell,[32] and the latter, on his arrival in Uganda, signed an addition to the 1900 Agreement which embodied most of the requests made by Kasagama and his supporters.[33]

The land question was to remain a source of grievance for many years, but Kasagama was now in a more powerful position than he had even been. On 16 March 1908, in a great ceremony in Kabarole, the Rev. G. R. Blackledge placed the crown upon the Mukama's head for the first time, thus symbolically linking Kasagama's triumph with the success of the Church Missionary Society. As the Mukama left his palace, drums sounded and the people shouted his praises. In the *Rukurato* hall Kasagama took his seat and welcomed his European guests to what he described as a traditional ceremony, though once again the tradition came from Bunyoro rather than from the newly created Kingdom of Toro. In the evening there was dancing and feasting and a demonstration of the ancient arts of war.[34] Kasagama had come into his own and he proudly surveyed his achievements. He was ruler not, it is true, of the old Empire of Bunyoro-Kitara, but of a kingdom which he could with some truth call his own. The British had provided the framework but the building was Kasagama's. It rested securely upon the twin foundations of British support and Bunyoro tradition. The people might grumble under the weight of the Mukama's authority, but many of them had inherited a tradition of subjugation to Banyoro rulers and thus had little inclination for revolt. In any case, they now believed that Kasagama's regime had the blessing of the Protectorate Administration. As far as the chiefs were concerned, their loyalty was assured by their being allowed to make extortionate demands upon their people, and by Kasagama's insistence that they should spend a considerable amount of their time in Kabarole where he could keep a close watch upon them.[35] Needless to say, Protectorate officials did not approve of this latter arrangement because they believed the chiefs would be better employed administering their *sazas*, but they cautiously refrained from interference.

In his attitude towards the Protectorate authorities Kasagama also showed a new confidence which the British were soon to describe as arrogance. In the years immediately following the signing of the 1900 Agreement the Mukama's behaviour had, on the whole, been defensive. In 1901, for example, Mr H. M. Tarrant, acting-collector in Toro, had complained that Kasagama and his chiefs were deliberately preventing the peasantry from making contact with Protectorate officials for fear of losing their hold over them.[36] Two years later Mr S. Ormsby remarked that the Mukama always insisted that the peasantry should give up 'bad old customs', but firmly upheld traditional rights when it was proposed to get rid of any custom, no matter how unjust, which he believed to contribute to his personal authority. Moreover, whenever the collector wished to summon a *baraza* in order to discuss these matters Kasagama was quick to feign illness and to beg to be excused attendance.[37] By 1908 such subterfuges had ceased to be necessary and Kasagama rejoiced in the exercise of power.

The Mukama's assertiveness owed its success to a number of factors. Pride of place must be given to his own personal qualities, his energy, his determination and his resolution, and above all his unswerving adherence to an authoritarian concept of the role of the Mukama. All these qualities were given a freer rein as the result of the rapid turnover among Protectorate officials in the kingdom in the formative years at the beginning of the century. Collectors, and later district commissioners as they came to be called, held office for only a few months and rarely for more than a year, while sub-commissioners, later provincial commissioners, fared little better. Between 1908 and 1912 there was, indeed, no provision in the estimates for a provincial commissioner for the Western Province.

In addition, the concept of indirect rule which was stressed by George Wilson as early as 1905[38] combined with Kasagama's own durability to make his position almost impregnable. Indirect rule, as Sir Philip Mitchell was later to point out, was no more than a means to an end, but in view of the limited resources at the disposal of the Protectorate Administration, it was an expedient which could not be lightly rejected. To administer a country through the traditional agencies of government was not only an economy but was also, provided those agencies were prepared to cooperate, less likely to arouse hostility or misunderstanding than would the direct intervention of alien officials. In the early years of the Protectorate the main concern of the Administration was to maintain peace and order and to develop a competent system of local government, and for this limited purpose Kasagama had seemed an excellent tool. The difficulties which had arisen were due to the failure of Protectorate officials to realize that the countries of Africa were inhabited by dynamic societies where change was constantly taking place, so that any attempt to impose a static system was bound to result in conflict.

More friction would occur later when the Protectorate Administration attempted to advance to the second stage of indirect rule by introducing new ideas of development, but until the outbreak of the First World War Toro was protected to a considerable extent by its geographical situation from many of the changes which were affecting Buganda and parts of the Eastern Province. Sir Hesketh Bell and his successor, Sir Frederick Jackson, pressed for an extension of the Uganda Railway westward as far as Kampala and then on to link up with the Belgian Congo railway system and the grand design of the Cape to Cairo Railway, but financial support was lacking. Even the roads could not be kept in good enough repair to meet the needs of the steadily increasing motor traffic. In wet weather the rich, rust-red soil was quickly churned into mud, and even in the dry season swamps provided a hazard to motor vehicles. Although a few European coffee planters took up residence in the vicinity of Fort Portal, the cotton boom which affected both chiefs and peasantry in Buganda and the Eastern Province did not penetrate to Toro. In a moment of official optimism a branch of the Treasury Savings Bank, founded to encourage Africans to save their money in European fashion, was opened in Fort Portal in 1909, but the Batoro preferred to invest in cattle and goats, while the Indian traders who had opened their tiny all-purpose shops in Toro were prepared to offer far higher rates of interest than those proposed by the Government Bank. European-style education was, however, just beginning to make its way into the kingdom, pioneered by missionaries. The White Fathers, as well as the C.M.S., had opened schools, and although the number of children in attendance numbered only hundreds by 1914[39] the importance of this development for the future of the kingdom was far from insignificant.

The attitude of the Protectorate authorities towards the missionaries had changed over the years. Harassed officials had never taken kindly to the rivalry between the missionary societies nor had they wholly approved of the way in which the C.M.S. agents had taken Kasagama's part in disputes with the Protectorate Administration. The Rev. A. B. Fisher, in particular, had angered officials and in 1897 Captain Sitwell had threatened to resign if Fisher were allowed to return to Toro. Even Sir Harry Johnston, who disliked missionary intervention in 'government', reflected official opinion when he referred to him in 1900 as a '*mtu mbaya sana*' (a very bad/troublesome man). It was shortly after this that Fisher came to blows with a member of the Catholic mission over the religious affiliation of the young chief Bulemu of Kitagwenda,[40] and early in the following year he annoyed the acting-collector, Mr Tarrant, by complaining that the latter had abused the Mukama and his chiefs and had scolded them for being Christians.[41] Tarrant was extremely critical of the work of Kasagama and his chiefs and doubtless atributed some of their arrogance and lack of consideration for the peasantry to the high opinion of themselves which the C.M.S. missionaries had encouraged. Mr Wylde, too, who was collector in Toro at the end of 1901, had become so exasperated by Fisher's behaviour that he asked for him to be removed from the district, a recommendation which received the hearty endorsement of the Sub-Commissioner for the Western Province, Stephen Bagge, who added a rider that Fisher's expulsion should be from the entire Province.[42]

Although Fisher was probably a more explosive character than any of his colleagues, he only reflected in extreme measure the tension which in the early days had existed between the two parties of missionaries, each determined to promote its interests and each convinced that this could be most effectively and appropriately achieved through bolstering the authority of the indigenous chiefs. The White Fathers, believing their rivals to be at an advantage in dealing with the Protectorate authorities because of their British origins, were anxious to demand equal treatment and were convinced that official attempts to secure this equality would be thwarted by Kasagama and his C.M.S. allies. R. Baile, collector in 1900, protested to his friend, the Special Commissioner, Sir Harry Johnston, that although he had appointed a Roman Catholic chief as a second *katikkiro* to represent his faction's interests at the court, the White Fathers had asked him to rescind his decision. This apparently strange behaviour was, however, due to the fact that it was Kasagama himself who had selected the chief in question.[43]

That the Mukama was suspicious of the loyalty of the Catholic chiefs was beyond doubt, and his knowledge of the divisions which could be caused by religious differences within a kingdom was based upon the bitter experience of the neighbouring state of Buganda. He was consequently unwilling to appoint any Catholic chief who was prepared to stand up to him lest this should indicate a challenge to his sovereignty. Few would dare to take the risk, and one who did, Leo Tibagwa, chief of Bunyangabo, was falsely accused of carrying a knife with which he planned to kill the Mukama and was deprived of his office, while Kasagama took possession of his cattle, sheep and goats.[44]

By the end of the first decade of the twentieth century this unhappy situation had greatly improved. With the growing stability within the kingdom the tension between the missionary societies was reduced, while the Protectorate authorities were beginning to recognize that the missionaries' zeal was not necessarily destructive but might serve both the kingdom and the Protectorate well.

Kasagama's first serious clash with the Protectorate Administration after the unhappy days of Captain Ashburnham occurred in 1912. The *saza* chief of Mwenge, Zakaria Kalema, was dismissed on the district commissioner's order in spite of protests from the Mukama. The charge was one of general incompetence and in particular of Kalema's involvement with a

European ivory poacher. The *saza* chief of Burahya, together with the *saza* chief of Kitagwenda – none other than Nasanairi Mugurusi, the *katikkiro* – were also threatened with dismissal for incompetence.[45] The Governor, Sir Frederick Jackson, took the opportunity offered by a visit to Fort Portal in February to castigate the Mukama and his chiefs orally for their conceit and for their lack of interest in the people. Ever resilient, however, Kasagama in his turn complained that the Protectorate officials did not show him adequate respect. Jackson was unsympathetic but the incident to which Kasagama particularly referred, an occasion when he had been ordered by the district commissioner to stand when a police officer entered the room, must have appeared to the Mukama as a serious indignity, and his anger was quickened by an anxiety to maintain his status vis-à-vis the Protectorate Administration.

These incidents marked the beginning of a period of friction between Kasagama and various officials. Only a few months later another chief, a relative of Kasagama, was dismissed for embezzling poll tax money, and once again the Mukama tried to protect the culprit. Having failed, he even agreed to keep the chieftainship open for the offender's son, who at the time was only eleven years old. The Governor was exasperated and took the significant step of himself appointing a Muganda chief to the vacant office. This was a bitter blow to Kasagama, and not only to his pride as the Governor believed, but to his concept of sovereignty within the kingdom. His reaction to the news was predictably explosive and after a vigorous oral exchange with the provincial commissioner he was summoned to Entebbe, where Jackson berated him and recalled the distasteful and now almost forgotten fact that the Mukama owed his kingdom to Captain Lugard.

It is not insignificant, however, that in spite of this clash there was no suggestion that Kasagama should be deposed. The Protectorate officials had now come to accept him as the traditional ruler of his country, a man to be threatened, cajoled or encouraged, but not to be removed. Even while the disputes were taking place, in 1912, a new judicial agreement was signed between the Protectorate Administration and the Mukama and his chiefs and was brought into operation in 1913. The new arrangements followed upon the promulgation in 1911 of the Courts Ordinance which provided for the supervision by British courts of any native courts set up under the ordinance. The new agreement empowered the Mukama, subject to the consent of the Governor, to set up courts of his own devising in order to try cases between natives of the district and to define the limits of their jurisdiction. The Governor might also authorize such courts to try natives of the Protectorate who were not Batoro.[46]

The outbreak of the First World War in 1914 provided a respite in the growing tension between Kasagama and the Protectorate authorities. The Mukama was active in the recruitment of men for the army and carrier services and was made an M.B.E. for his efforts.[47] But when the war ended Kasagama concentrated his efforts once again upon controlling his own kingdom. The debate, some of it heated, which was aroused between 1919 and 1921 by the creation of a Uganda Legislative Council with only three unofficial members – two Europeans and one Asian – passed Toro by. The Government of Buganda scrutinized the proposals and came to the positive conclusion that they wished to have no part in the Council to which, in any case, they had not been invited to send a representative. Kasagama, by contrast, simply ignored the whole issue which in his view did not concern his kingdom. He had enough worries at home. The land question remained unsettled and Protectorate officials were once again beginning to interfere in the affairs of the district.

To the British administrators Kasagama's insistence on keeping authority in his own hands appeared obstructive. They saw in his relations with his chiefs a conspiracy to exploit the peasantry to their own ends. Mikairi Rusoke, who had succeeded Mugurusi as *katikkiro* in 1914, they described as deceitful and cunning, and Sir Robert Coryndon, who became Governor of Uganda in 1917, found it necessary to warn Kasagama that if the situation in the kingdom did not improve Rusoke would be replaced by a Muganda *katikkiro*. Coryndon, however, appears to have been uncertain how to deal with the Mukama himself. In an attempt to put greater pressure upon him he threatened to report him to the Colonial Secretary,[48] though what would be the outcome of such action was far from clear. So successfully had Kasagama established himself as hereditary ruler of Toro that it would have been difficult to find a replacement for him in spite of the provisions of the 1900 Agreement.

Sir Geoffrey Archer, Coryndon's successor, determined to employ new tactics. The reports from Toro about Kasagama's performance were still unfavourable so Archer summoned the Mukama and his *katikkiro* to Entebbe in 1923. Rusoke was dismissed as Coryndon had threatened he would be, but Kasagama saw that he did not suffer unduly. He was appointed chief of Kibale, a *saza* which was at the same time enlarged by the inclusion of the former county of Kitagwenda, though it was a clear indication of the growing importance of the office of Mukama that Rusoke's transfer from a post which in 1900 had been regarded as purely advisory to that of *saza* chief was now regarded as demotion.[49] He was replaced as *katikkiro* for a two-year term by the Muganda *saza* chief of Singo, Nasanairi Mayanja. Archer, however, was instinctively sympathetic towards Kasagama himself. He saw him as the ruler of what he automatically referred to as the Mukama's 'country' and looked upon his own role less as that of Governor in an executive sense than as supervisor and guide to the African monarchs. Although he could not avoid contrasting unfavourably the developments in Toro with those in other districts he believed Kasagama's authority must be upheld. It was on this account, and in the hope of giving the Mukama a fresh start, that he recalled the district commissioner, Mr C. E. E. Sullivan, who had supported the Toro peasantry against what he himself believed to be extortion and oppression by the Mukama and his chiefs.[50]

In spite of the appointment of a Muganda *katikkiro*, therefore, Sullivan's recall appeared to be a vindication of Kasagama's authority, more particularly since it was widely believed that Sullivan had been reprimanded by the Governor. The Mukama was now convinced that he was fully accepted by the Protectorate authorities for the king he believed himself to be. The C.M.S. missionaries were delighted, agreeing with Kasagama that this was a moment of triumph. Reflecting upon their jubilation, however, a sceptical provincial commissioner recalled the days of adversity, a quarter of a century earlier, which Kasagama and the missionaries now seemed to have forgotten. And forgotten they certainly were. If the British were prepared to create the illusion of a traditional kingdom, Kasagama was willing to convert that illusion into reality and to fill it with the symbols of monarchy which the situation demanded.

In the state of euphoria created by these events the Mukama threw himself more enthusiastically into the duties expected of him by the Protectorate Administration. But he was not yet wholly satisfied. A complaisant Governor was no doubt an asset, but the Government's attitude towards the land question remained unresolved. The initial delays occasioned by the desire to provide an equitable arrangement for the whole Protectorate had been extended by the disagreement between those who wished to encourage European settlement by making land readily available to planters and those officials who wished to protect the interests of the African population. After lengthy debate it was finally agreed that grants of land in Toro should be limited to those already made by the 1900 Agreement, and in an attempt to avoid the possibility of abuse in the future a scheme was adopted in 1923 which, while protecting the right of the *Mukama* and his leading chiefs to receive their ten per cent 'tribute', aimed to provide fixed salaries for lesser chiefs. To finance the undertaking the Toro Government's revenue from all sources, including the income from the salt trade hitherto accruing to Kasagama and in lieu of which he was now made an annual payment, was placed in a common fund and a subsidy was granted by the Protectorate Administration to set the plan in motion. Instead of paying tribute, everyone other than the chiefs holding private estates under the Agreement would be required in future to contribute to the central fund an annual sum of six shillings as rent for the land they occupied.

The new arrangements unfortunately did not take into account the fact that for more than a quarter of a century Kasagama had been exercising what he believed to be his right as Mukama by making grants of land to his friends along with the attendant benefits in tribute payable in money, labour, food or beer. This, it is true, was contrary to the terms of the 1900 Agreement, but as Kasagama had frequently pointed out he had no other means of remunerating lesser chiefs for their services or of rewarding his supporters for their assistance. Nor was the policy which he had adopted wholly without benefit to the peasants themselves. They were accustomed to paying tribute to chiefs in return for protection and in earlier times even the independent Batoro would not have survived for long without such guarantees. Accustomed to the vagaries of their overlords the peasants had not, for the most part, regarded the demands made upon them by Kasagama's chiefs as excessive. The new arrangements, therefore, left the Mukama and his chiefs disgruntled while any hope the Protectorate Administration may have had of satisfying the demands of the peasantry was destroyed by the tactless issue of the same tickets as receipts for rent as were already in use for Crown land rent receipts. Not unnaturally the peasants assumed that this meant their land had been surreptitiously annexed by the Protectorate authorities. A new form of receipt was introduced as soon as the mistake was recognized but the damage had been done.

The discontent of the Batoro came to a head in 1926. As the provincial commissioner, Mr P. W. Cooper, was about to go on leave in February of that year Kasagama and his chiefs presented him with a letter in which it was said that he was leaving nothing behind but trouble and that they hoped he would not return.[51] The Governor, Sir William Gowers, at once summoned Kasagama to Entebbe and he and his chiefs were fined. Yet even now the Mukama's position was not challenged. Instead, a committee of enquiry consisting of two officials, Mr C. E. E. Sullivan and Mr H. B. Thomas, was asked to investigate the grievances of the people of Toro.

In their report the committee admitted that the 1900 Agreement was vague and indefinite on many points and that the arrangements made in 1923 were not very sympathetic towards traditional attitudes regarding the control of land. They therefore suggested amendments which coincided more closely with the practice already adopted by Kasagama, while agreeing that to a detached observer they might appear to be favouring members of a ruling family who rendered relatively little service to the kingdom. The committtee then looked at the question of the salt lakes. Taking the view that some surrender of traditional sovereignty had been implicit even in the arrangements made by Lugard in 1891 and that this was justifiable on the ground that Kasagama had received British protection in return, they nevertheless thought it might soften the blow the Mukama had received in 1922 when the annual lease of the salt lakes was terminated if an announcement were made guaranteeing him £100 a year from the salt revenue as long as the money was available. The third point upon which the committee commented was the status of Bwamba. Kasagama had consistently protested that under the terms of the 1900 Agreement this area formed part of Toro and that the omission of any reference to it in 1906 was simply an oversight. The committee now proposed a compromise under the terms of which the Mukama would be entitled to mark out a limited area of official land in Bwamba; but no private estates would be granted since, quite obviously, the Batoro had owned none in the area in 1900.[52]

The committee's recommendations were approved by the Secretary of State and promulgated in 1927.[53] Kasagama, however, lived only briefly to savour their implications. He died on 31 December 1928 while touring Mwenge. He had never been popular there, for the inhabitants were Banyoro who disliked his domineering manner and had little sympathy for the concept of a Toro Kingdom. Not surprisingly there were rumours that the Mukama had been poisoned but they were never substantiated. The fact that they even existed, however, is indicative of the controversial position Kasagama had occupied in the affairs of his kingdom. Toro was virtually his own creation and he had created it in the image he had inherited from his Babito forebears. But he had failed to win the hearts of all his subjects and although he was a descendant of the ruling house of Bunyoro, on the score of Kaboyo's rebellion and his own restoration at the hands of Lugard he could lay no claim to divine right of succession as a means of capturing his subjects' loyalty. Even the chiefs who had gained so much from their adherence to the Mukama had given their support either to satisfy their cupidity or from respect, rather than from affection.

Yet, in spite of the difficulties he had faced, Kasagama had remained true to his own concept of monarchy. Through his association with the Church Missionary Society he had introduced a measure of westernization in his kingdom but in a manner which in his own lifetime avoided any challenge to traditional authority. For their part, although the C.M.S. brought revolutionary ideas to the country they did so under the shadow of established authority because they believed their teaching could only bear fruit in a society where peace and order prevailed and where the people were protected from material and emotional exploitation by European adventurers. The protective role adopted by the missionaries and Kasagama's own determination to preserve the status of the monarchy meant that even the location of the district and later of the provincial headquarters at Fort Portal, close beside his own capital in Kabarole, did not impinge markedly upon the Mukama's way of life. From his hilltop residence he looked out upon the fertile land which he had made into a kingdom and was deeply satisfied with his achievement.

Nor, in his own opinion, had Kasagama caused his kingdom to suffer by limiting its external contacts. He had in no way resisted the arrival of European planters who were attracted to Toro by the prospect of growing coffee in such superb surroundings, but he had ensured that they would be in no position to influence the affairs of the country unduly, even if they had wished to do so. Indian traders, too, had been permitted to open their shops in Fort Portal and other trading centres throughout the kingdom and had been made welcome because they brought goods which the people desired. His relations with Protectorate officials had been mixed, but until the outbreak of the First World War administrators had been mainly concerned with the maintenance of order and the collection of taxes and had therefore found it necessary to rely upon Kasagama and his chiefs in order to achieve these objectives. Even when the propaganda levelled against Germany as a colonial power had forced the other powers after the war to reconsider their own obligations to the African peoples they administered, the new ideal of trusteeship which emerged from their thinking embodied the spirit of conservatism rather than kindling a reforming zeal. Mr Sullivan might accuse the Mukama and chiefs of ignoring the well-being of their subjects, but for most British administrators monarchy was monarchy and should not be too casually subverted.

In any case, with the arrival of the planters and with opportunities elsewhere in the Protectorate the peasants were already beginning to find a new source of independence. The old practice of 'diffidation' which had led dissatisfied subjects to seek their fortune beyond the borders of the kingdom was being rapidly replaced by a new type of exodus. While a few gained employment with the coffee planters within the kingdom others sought more varied adventures in other parts of the Protectorate and particularly in the commercial capital of Kampala. They became servants in European households or messengers in trading companies and even, if they had a little education, might aspire to more exalted employment as minor clerks in government offices. These men did not take their families with them, preferring to leave wives and children at home to tend their crops so that any wages they might be paid would, apart from the cost of their own maintenance, be clear profit. Although this meant some loss of manpower to the kingdom the financial return in the form of taxes to some extent made up for it and Kasagama was not dissatisfied. He left to his successor a strong tradition of government and a kingdom capable of achieving great prosperity.

V · The Kingdom Looks Outward

George Kamrasi Rukidi, who succeeded Kasagama in 1929, resembled his father in many respects. Like his predecessor the young Mukama was physically a big man and his service with the King's African Rifles had strengthened his inherited power of command. He possessed the same single-minded determination which had enabled Kasagama to triumph over difficulties and he had the same uncompromising view of monarchy. To these austere qualities were added a sense of humour and a deep humanity which, in time, were to make it possible for Rukidi to come closer to his people than his father had ever done. Blended into his character there were, in addition, two contrasting elements which were to make him more influential in the affairs of Uganda as a whole than his position as the head of a tiny kingdom would have justified. He was endowed with the sort of simplicity which sees to the heart of things and at the same time he had an instinctive appreciation of people's reactions which in another man might have seemed like cunning.

When he came to the throne – or as the ruling family of Toro, proud of the independence brought by Kaboyo, preferred to say, when he 'rebelled' – Rukidi was young and inexperienced but he was anxious to show himself as a true Mukama. The presence of a Muganda *katikkiro* and two Baganda *saza* chiefs in Bwamba and Mwenge both irked him and offended his pride. Yosia Sewali was the third Muganda to hold the office of *katikkiro* of Toro and was highly regarded by Protectorate officials. The first Muganda *katikkiro*, Nasanairi Mayanja, fell ill within a year of his appointment and was succeeded by Rauli Kiwanuka. He, too, did not stay long. After eighteen months he left Toro in May 1926 to become *saza* chief in his own kingdom, in Buddu. Yosia Sewali had therefore had a year and a half in which to take the measure of Toro before Rukidi became Mukama, which put the young man at a disadvantage. For this among other reasons, including the desire to demonstrate his independence, Rukidi tended to seek advice from his own people rather than from the *katikkiro*.

It was a further blow to his prestige and to that of his chiefs when the right to levy tribute, which had been regularized in 1923, was removed six years later. Now tribute was to be collected as part of the poll tax from which refunds would be made to the native administration on the assumption that the tribute had been intended for the support of the local government. To Rukidi local government was no impersonal abstraction; local government meant himself and his chiefs, and the diversion of the tribute from their pockets to the local treasury implied a diminution in their status in the eyes of the people. He protested to the Protectorate authorities regarding the new arrangement but to no avail, and it remained in force as a constant challenge to the Mukama's sense of justice.

The retirement of the two Baganda *saza* chiefs in 1932 was the occasion of an attempt by the Mukama to gain a closer control of affairs, but he was only partially successful. Kesi Mukasa was replaced as *saza* chief of Mwenge by the same Mikairi Rusoke who had been dismissed from the post of *katikkiro* in 1923, but even this move had its drawbacks. The Protectorate Administration now insisted that the *saza* of Kitagweta should be amalgamated with Mwenge and Nyakabimba with Kyaka, thus creating counties of a size which displeased Rukidi who did not like to see his chiefs wielding such extensive authority. His opposition to these changes having failed he was more successful in rejecting the absorption of the *saza* of Bunyangabo in the neighbouring county of Burahya, and he flatly refused to contemplate the transfer of part of Kibale to Ankole although the region in question, once a part of the semi-autonomous kingdom of Kitagwenda, had constantly resisted the sovereignty of successive Bakama of Toro.

Noting what he believed to be the obstinacy of the Mukama, the provincial commissioner of the Western Province commented that, 'Paramount chiefs are a costly luxury which Native Administrations can ill afford. Most of the work is done by the *katikkiro* and the Mukama would be glad to get rid of him.'[1] This was a misjudgement, for the Native Administration in Toro had grown up round the office of Mukama. Although local government could well have functioned without Rukidi it would have been the sort of alien institution which the presence of a Muganda *katikkiro* even now threatened that it might become. The retirement of Yosia Sewali in 1934 gave Rukidi an opportunity to show his metal and to restore to the monarchy the role for which he believed it to be fitted and for which the concept of indirect rule had made such generous provision in the time of his father. Sewali took six months' leave before quitting his post and in the interval before a successor was appointed the Mukama carried out the duties of *katikkiro* in addition to his own. This not only enabled him to gain a stronger grasp of the affairs of government but also to see the virtues of a proposal put before him by the district commissioner, who suggested that in future the duties of the *katikkiro* should be fulfilled by a *saza* chief or other suitable person at a salary of £250 a year, which was equal to the salary of the chief of Mwenge, the highest-paid among the *saza* chiefs at the time. The appointment would then be held for two years and might be renewed for further periods of two years if the man appointed proved suitable.

The district commissioner's object in making this proposal was to avoid excessive influence being attached to the post of *kitikkiro* which might arouse jealousy and rivalry among the other chiefs. Rukidi, however, saw at once that the new arrangement would strengthen his own hand in relation to his people but would make him more vulnerable to criticism by the Protectorate authorities if anything went wrong in Toro. It was a risk that he was prepared to take and he willingly appointed a promising young Mutoro, Yosama Mbaijama, *saza* chief of Bwamba, to the vacant post when his own six months' tenure of office was completed.

The Protectorate authorities were happy with the new *katikkiro* but were not without reservations about the effects of indirect rule in Toro. Early in 1934 the enterprising and eccentric district commissioner of Lango District, Captain J. E. T. Philipps, submitted a report containing serious criticisms of the Protectorate Administration's policy which, he claimed, had encouraged chiefs to oppress the peasantry in a variety of ways. The Governor was sufficiently impressed by the force of Philipps' arguments to circulate the report throughout the Protectorate with the request for comments about its relevance to other districts.

In reply the district commissioner of Toro, Mr I. H. B. Sandford, remarked that the Batoro were adept at making their displeasure felt if they believed they were being ill-treated by their chiefs. They were not averse to burning the houses of their oppressors, but since the incidence of crimes of this sort was extremely low it could be assumed that the peasantry of Toro were not unhappy with their rulers. He went on to add that the practice of demanding labour had been largely curbed by Protectorate officials and although nepotism and intrigue were rife, and while any refusal to accept the district commissioner's advice regarding appointments to the office of chief was regarded as a gesture of independence, the main criticism which could be levelled against the Mukama and his supporters was that they were inefficient rather than oppressive. He considered that the 1900 Agreement had played into the hands of the ruling family, and in a concise historical memorandum on the development of the kingdom since the time of Kaboyo he drew attention to the number of occasions when Protectorate officials had found it necessary to censure Kasagama. He argued that this was the result of a policy which had striven to maintain and extend the privileges of the Mukama and a small clique of his immediate dependants and that in consequence the people of Toro had no real sense of loyalty to their rulers. This was reflected in the apathy of the inhabitants of the kingdom and accounted for their failure to respond to the challenge presented by the opportunity to grow economic crops.

The Mukama appeared to justify Sandford's strictures when he presented a petition in August 1934 protesting that the practice of allocating official land to chiefs had been abandoned with a consequent loss of labour and other forms of tribute. The petition had been submitted in the hope that it would be handed to a group of British MPs who were touring Uganda as members of the Empire Parliamentary Association but who had not included Toro in their itinerary. The Mukama's request was not accepted, though once again his action had not sprung from a merely selfish desire to acquire wealth for himself and his chiefs. Sandford, like many of his predecessors, believed that the Protectorate Administration had behaved generously towards the Mukama and his father and could not understand why, instead of showing gratitude, they accepted every concession as if it were their right.

Rukidi, however, no less than Kasagama, refused to see himself in any other role than that of hereditary ruler of Toro. Like his predecessor he believed that the extension of the kingdom at the expense of Bunyoro had been the fruit of Kasagama's initiative and was justified, as the rule of the former Bakama of Bunyoro had been, by a mixture of hereditary right and military strength. The Protectorate Administration had simply recognized a *de jure* as well as a *de facto* situation, and Rukidi had no desire to probe more deeply into the nature of the relationship between the Kingdom and the Protectorate authorities. That the latter had certain powers and interests which could not, indeed should not, be challenged he was prepared to admit, but that those powers or interests should interfere with the rights of the ruler of Toro he was not prepared to concede. When, as in 1923, Protectorate officials had imposed a new system for collecting taxes and paying chiefs it could only be regarded as an aberration which justice must in time set to rights. Hence his constant plea for a reversion to the earlier position. In face of such obduracy Protectorate officials wavered between exasperation and resignation and the result was that the rulers tended to be left to pursue their own plans so long as they did not clash openly with British policy.

This situation was clearly reflected in the reaction of the provincial commissioner, Mr W. G. Adams, to Sandford's résumé of the history of Toro. He ruefully agreed that indirect rule had been carried too far in Toro and regretted that the opportunity had not been taken in 1926 to suspend the Agreement on the ground that Kasagama had failed to show the loyalty which was rightly demanded of him. He recognized, however, that the moment had passed and tried to console himself with the admission that the Mukama appeared to be showing a more cooperative attitude towards the Protectorate Administration now that the Muganda *katikkiro* had left.

Adams' guarded optimism was soon to receive a setback. In 1936 a new Governor, Sir Philip Mitchell, attempted to clarify the relations between Toro and the Protectorate Administration. A number of minor agreements had been signed at different times to straighten out and expand the arrangements contained in the original 1900 Agreement. Mitchell's view was that a new, more comprehensive agreement, along the lines of one recently signed by the Mukama of Bunyoro, would help to avoid difficulties in the future. Rukidi, however, was wary of the proposal. He disliked intensely an arrangement which appeared to perpetuate the recent changes concerning tribute, and an offer to reduce the poll tax levied on his subjects seemed an unacceptable *quid pro quo*. The district commissioner, like most other officials who had had dealings with the Mukama, attributed the latter's reaction to a lack of concern for his people and an exaggerated interest in his own financial gains. Once again, however, Rukidi argued that, whatever the attractions of tribute as a source of income, it was as a symbol of his authority that he cherished it. Moreover, the draft of the agreement presented to Rukidi referred to him throughout as the 'Ruling Chief', and although the use of this term contained no sinister implications it was ill-judged. The Mukama's hopes were set on acquiring the title of 'His Highness' enjoyed by the Kabaka of Buganda since the signing of the 1900 Buganda Agreement while the title which now seemed to have been proposed for him would have reduced him to the position he had occupied before the 1906 amendment to the Agreement. Caustically Rukidi enquired if there was any intention of amending the Buganda Agreement and, if not, why there was any necessity to change the Toro Agreement.

Sir Philip Mitchell had had lengthy experience of the operation of indirect rule in Tanganyika and on arriving in Uganda had been distressed by the almost mystical reverence with which the concept was regarded by many government officers. Within a year of his appointment as Governor, and less than a month before he presented his proposals for a revision of the Toro Agreement, he had taken advantage of an invitation to address the Uganda Society to expound his own views upon what seemed to have become the foundation stone of Britain's colonial administration. 'Indirect Rule,' he said,

> is no more than a means to an end. . . . It has no intrinsic value in itself, and it follows that, if it fails to achieve its end judged by reasonable standards, it has nothing to be said for it . . . it is certainly not anything to do with sovereignty, home-rule, nationalism and the like; these are matters of political principle. It may or may not be right for one race or nation to rule another, but, whether it is or whether it is not, it has nothing to do with administrative systems.[2]

If this had been the sum total of Mitchell's views he might

have been more uncompromising than his predecessors had been in his dealings with traditional African authorities who proved obdurate. But he could not escape his own background. Trained in the art of handling African problems by Sir Donald Cameron, the leading exponent of indirect rule in East Africa, and troubled by a highly developed intellect which enabled him to see many sides to every question, Mitchell was no more competent to act decisively towards Toro than those who had gone before him. Although he recognized that indirect rule, like any other form of administration, would eventually be judged only by results, he was still convinced that it was the only satisfactory means available for a foreign power which wished to govern by cooperation rather than by compulsion. Characteristically he argued that to rely upon indigenous institutions did not imply an excessive reverence for tradition for its own sake. But although societies must change, that change could best be accomplished through the agency of the corporate will embodied in traditional authority.

Revolutionary action could scarcely spring from such a measured appraisal of the situation. Nor did it. Mitchell's response to two months' procrastination on the part of the Mukama over the proposal for a revision of the Agreement was to withdraw the scheme and instead to try to achieve his aims by less controversial administrative action. Even then his plan was not entirely pleasing to the Mukama, particularly in so far as it clearly put an end to the collection of tribute. In its place rent was to be collected by landowners from tenants on their private estates on conditions laid down by the land office and only with the Governor's approval. The element of tribute would be absorbed in the poll tax.

Mitchell offered the Mukama an interview to discuss the new arrangement and this took place at Entebbe in December 1936. As anticipated, Rukidi once more stressed the importance of tribute as a symbol of loyalty to the properly constituted authority and denied that by his persistence he was disregarding the well-being of his people. He pointed out with some truth that the peasants did not object to paying tribute and that the earlier arrangement by which it had been collected in the form of a tax had been approved by the Protectorate Administration and had virtually become part of the original Agreement. Mitchell, somewhat surprisingly in view of his respect for indirect rule, was unimpressed by these arguments, possibly because he had received reports that Rukidi had again been behaving badly towards his people. Impatiently the Governor turned upon the Mukama and with uncharacteristic vehemence stated that the latter was not in treaty relationship with the King of England nor was his position in any way comparable to that of the Kabaka of Buganda. He was merely a chief, ruling over a small portion of the Protectorate by consent of His Majesty, and if that consent were withdrawn he would cease to rule.

Mitchell's outburst not only reflected his own exasperation, which was of a transitory nature, but also revealed a fundamental change in the British attitude towards agreements since the Toro Agreement had been signed in 1900. While the Toro Agreement had stated that failure by any of the chiefs to observe its terms might lead to withdrawal of Britain's recognition and the substitution of any alternative type of administration which might be thought necessary, Sir Harry Johnston had intended that this should simply be a warning to Kasagama that loyalty was expected of him. For Mitchell now to say that Rukidi ruled only by the consent of the King of England was, moreover, contrary to everything that had happened in Toro since 1900. But the sanctity of agreements with African chiefs had steadily been eroded during the first thirty years of the twentieth century by the joint action of administrative necessity and legal scrutiny. Reluctantly at first, but with increasing confidence, British official opinion had adopted the view that a Protecting Power was free to interpret agreements as it thought fit. This was an opinion which administrative officers serving in colonial dependencies and protectorates were less willing than their masters to accept, however, and although Mitchell's anger had led him to speak harsh words to Rukidi, both his earlier experience and his keen perception of the difficulties which might lie ahead encouraged him to act less ruthlessly than his remarks might have led the Mukama to expect. Consequently, having vented his righteous indignation the Governor took no further action.

All too soon more fearful problems were to face not only Toro but the whole world with the outbreak of the Second World War in 1939. Whatever the Mukama's hopes, Toro was now to be drawn irrevocably into a wider field of action. Two other events had already occurred in the same year which, in combination, served to mark the end of an era for the kingdom. First, the Western and Northern Provinces were amalgamated to form an enlarged Western Province and the provincial headquarters were transferred from Fort Portal to Masindi in Bunyoro. Although the moving of the headquarters was intended only to bring it into a more central geographical position, the effect was to shift the spotlight from events in Kabarole and provide a welcome respite for the Mukama. Second, and of a more symbolic character, was the retirement of Mikairi Rusoke, *saza* chief of Mwenge. Rusoke, the former *katikkiro* dismissed in 1923 by Governor Archer as part of the latter's contribution to the attempt to curb the powers of the rulers of Toro, had been associated with the monarchical establishment since the beginning of the century. He had been a signatory of the 1900 Agreement and had seen Kasagama build up his authority both with the aid of, and in spite of, British intervention. As *saza* chief at different times of Busongora, Kibale, Nyakabimba, Burahya and Mwenge, as well as *katikkiro*, he had constantly worked to support his overlord. His career had followed the pattern created by Kasagama for a closely knit group of his followers who held most of the important appointments in the kingdom in rotation, but were moved around sufficiently frequently to ensure that they did not get too strong a hold upon any one region.

Against this coterie of Kasagama's hand-picked men British efforts to influence developments had made only slow progress. Perhaps the greatest success had been achieved by missionaries, both Catholic and Protestant. Nevertheless, although the Protestants had been Kasagama's favourites he had undoubtedly benefited more from making use of their support than they had ever done from his benevolence. On more than one occasion they had almost despaired of making any lasting impression upon the Batoro, whom they regarded as fickle and sadly lacking in firmness of purpose. Yet the missionaries had persevered, particularly in their attempts to introduce a Christian and Western form of education into the kingdom, and by 1939 each society had a secondary school for boys in the vicinity of Fort Portal. The C.M.S. had 56 students at Nyakasura and the White Fathers had 37 at Virika. These figures, small though they were, were no worse than those of the mission schools elsewhere in the Protectorate outside the Kingdom of Buganda. The same, too, could be said of the progress in primary education where the Roman Catholics had 377 boys and 135 girls in full primary schools and 218 boys and 54 girls in vernacular primary schools. The Protestants had only one full primary school for boys with 83 pupils, and 387 boys and 107 girls in vernacular primary schools. The Protectorate authorities had not entered into competition with the missionary societies and there were only four government primary schools in the whole of Uganda.[3] They had, however, given financial aid to approved mission schools since 1906 when a grant had been made to King's School, Budo, and had subsequently committed themselves to a policy of assisting mission schools which reached a sufficiently high standard of competence. Governor Sir Geoffrey Archer had given a considerable impetus to education in the 1920s but Buganda had been the main beneficiary and no great change had taken place in Toro.

In a district where the incidence of malaria was high, the opening of eleven sub-dispensaries by the Protectorate medical department in the inter-war years in trading centres as far apart as Bundibugyo in Bwamba and Katwe in Busongora had provided an important service. The response of the population was surprisingly enthusiastic for a people normally apathetic about the work of the Protectorate Administration. In the course of 1939 no fewer than 66,000 new cases of one sort or another received attention.[4] In most other respects, however, the Batoro had remained indifferent to the siren song with which the Protectorate authorities sought to induce them to embrace a more progressive policy. The agricultural department, for example, encountered little enthusiasm, save in Bwamba, for its attempts to encourage the growing of economic crops. At the outbreak of war only 8000 acres of land were devoted to cotton-growing, mainly in the eastern portion of the kingdom. The majority of the population could satisfy most of their requirements from the rich soil of their own gardens, and if extra money were needed it could be obtained with greater certainty than cotton-growing could offer by working for European coffee planters around Fort Portal or, better still – since it provided a richer variety of opportunity – by seeking paid employment in Buganda and especially among the urban attractions of Kampala. In Bwamba in the 1930s the department of agriculture had managed to arouse interest in coffee-growing, however, and the hardy robusta variety was beginning to show promise of providing a new source of income to a people more inclined to stay at home than to wander at large in other parts of the Protectorate.

With the outbreak of war Toro's introspection and indifference to what was going on in the wider world were deeply disturbed. The sharp increase in prices offered for agricultural produce provided a greater incentive to cultivation than had the earlier exhortations of Protectorate officials, and the opportunities for paid employment in the services encouraged a number of younger men to shake off their lethargy and seek adventure further afield. At first, recruitment to the armed forces was slow, but under the vigorous persuasion of the Mukama large numbers eventually came forward, to serve in the Pioneer Corps and the Labour Battalions if not in the fighting units. Simultaneously the demand for cotton resulted in a rapid expansion of the area under cultivation to 19,400 acres in 1941 and even caused a decline in coffee production in Bwamba because it was thought that cotton offered better financial prospects. The cotton boom in fact proved to be short-lived and the area under production steadied at about 10,000 acres. The Baamba perceived their mistake, and with the price for robusta coffee rising from 7 cents a pound in 1939 to 28 cents in 1943 the output reached record proportions of more than 300 tons; by the end of the war the acreage under coffee reached what the department of agriculture regarded as saturation level at 2190 acres. A new crop, rice, was also tried out in Bwamba in 1943, and in 1946, 250 tons were marketed. European planters were also growing tea and bringing the total of land leased by expatriots to 10,500 acres, while seven estates acquired earlier in the century were still held in freehold. European enterprise created a further demand for labour, and so did the brief reopening of the copper workings in the Ruwenzoris in 1944.

This increase in activity was unfortunately matched by the enforced reduction in many plans for development which the Protectorate authorities had hoped to put into effect. The number of European officials in the kingdom was reduced to the barest minimum and development projects were run down. In spite of the increased pressure on transport and communications the road system was not expanded, and owing to the labour shortage maintenance could not be kept at its proper level. Yet, taken all in all, Toro probably benefited more from the war than might have been expected. Nor were the fears expressed by administrative officers about the likely impact of the return of numbers of ex-servicemen with large sums of money paid to them on demobilization ever justified. Indeed, it was a matter of regret to officials that few soldiers appeared to use their temporary wealth to build themselves permanent houses. Apart from the acquisition of wives there was no clear evidence of how the money was spent. Like most civilians forced by circumstances to serve in a disciplined unit, removed from their families for several years, the Batoro ex-servicemen were glad to return to their homes and, after a brief period of celebration, to take up their lives again where they had left off. The ties of clan remained strong and loyalty to chiefs was unimpaired. The restlessness which administrative officers had anticipated was little in evidence and there was even some disappointment among officials that, although one hundred men applied for agricultural training in centres set up by the Administration, few others sought to put the training in responsibility they had acquired in the army to any purpose which might serve the development of the kingdom.[5]

The hope that Toro's own leaders would set an example of energy and imagination received a setback with the death in 1946 of Marko Kaboha, who had served as *katikkiro* for most of the war. The son of a former Bunyoro chief, Leo Kaboha, who after being dismissed from his post for his part in the disturbances which took place in the neighbouring kingdom in 1907 had later moved indomitably to Toro to become in due course *saza* chief of Kitagweta, Marko Kaboha had himself given many years of service to the kingdom. He had succeeded the Muganda, Kesi Mukasa, as *saza* chief of Burahya, and by his reliability had done much to restore the reputation of the chiefs of Toro in the eyes of the Protectorate officials. His success and his preferment were indicative of other changes in the kingdom, notably in the relations between the missions and the Mukama, for he was a Roman Catholic and a leading figure in his Church.

Kaboha's place was taken by Hosea Nkojo, and immediately administrative reforms were introduced with the creation of *saza* and *gombolola* (sub-county) councils. Once again, too, on

1 January 1947 Fort Portal became the seat of a Western Province reduced in size by the re-creation of the Northern Province but more alive to the new developments which were occupying the attention of the whole Protectorate.

The Mukama and his chiefs now cooperated freely with the Protectorate Administration's plans for developing the resources of the kingdom. Gone were the days of conflict between European officials and the Toro hierarchy. The Mukama, mature in years and confident of his authority, believed that his position would be strengthened more by association with the British than by a constant assertion of his independence, particularly if the control of new developments were kept firmly in his own hands. With a steadily growing population which reached 257,873 in 1948 and 274,076 by 1950, the kingdom moved forward into an era of economic growth. The cotton crop amounted to 1035 tons in 1947 and the acreage planted in 1948 doubled. The Bakonjo of Busongora were now also growing cotton on an increasing scale, while the production of robusta coffee by the Baamba in 1948 reached the highest level since the boom years of the earlier part of the war. For the first time the flow of money into the kingdom began to affect the social life of the people. Corrugated iron roofs replaced the more aesthetically pleasing and more traditional thatch and gave a greater permanency to buildings. Bicycles began to appear in greater numbers upon the roads, carrying enormous burdens of cotton to the ginneries, or else precarious passengers, and added a new range of hazards to the lives of the cyclists and to the nerves of motorists attempting to overtake them. Sewing machines in innumerable roadside shops poured out a colourful range of cotton clothes, while a variety of new gadgets and more specialized tools for domestic use helped to make life for the peasants a little easier and a little more sophisticated.

This increased prosperity came at an opportune time, for in 1949 the Protectorate Administration decided to change the system of direct taxation to enable local governments to take greater responsibility for their own affairs. Instead of a poll tax which varied from region to region according to the ability of each district to pay, there was to be a lower, uniform poll tax of six shillings. The local governments might then levy a native administration tax with which to develop and maintain certain local services. Although this was not the tribute for which the Mukama and his chiefs had so often pleaded, it was at least a step in that direction and provided an incentive to the local authorities to encourage the development of the kingdom's resources so as to make the people capable of paying higher taxes.

The peaceful progress in Toro in the years immediately following the war contrasted markedly with the tumultuous events in Buganda. There, by contrast, one section of the chiefs tried to take advantage of a situation in which the British authorities had recently reduced the level of their intervention in Buganda's affairs and in which a young and inexperienced Kabaka was making his first tentative efforts to take control of the country. In January 1945 rioting broke out near the Kabaka's capital and this was followed in September by the murder of Martin Nsibirwira, the *katikkiro*, as he left the cathedral on Namirembe Hill. Order was restored, but a feeling of restlessness and discontent persisted and encouraged a section of the population to resist any attempt by the Kabaka to cooperate with the Protectorate Administration. In Toro, however, Rukidi remained in calm control, his chiefs both unwilling and unable to challenge his authority and his popularity spreading steadily throughout the kingdom. In 1950 Toro could look backward with satisfaction and into the future with a fair degree of confidence. Festivities were held to mark the fiftieth anniversary of the Toro Agreement; among those who took part was Nasanairi Mugurusi who, as *saza* chief of Mwenge, had been a signatory to the Agreement although subsequently dismissed from the office of *katikkiro* on charges of corrupt dealings with European ivory poachers.

There were, however, indications that changes were about to take place which the Mukama would find it difficult to control. In the same year, 1950, the newly created Western Province Council in which Toro was represented met for the first time to elect a member to sit in the Protectorate Legislative Council. The Provincial Councils had been set up under the African Local Government Ordinance of 1949 and had aroused some consternation in the Western Province. They were to some extent the embodiment of the ideal first mentioned by George Wilson half a century earlier (see p. 94) – which might have made sense in 1900, when the upheaval consequent upon the civil war in Buganda and the overthrow of Kabarega had left the country uncertain about its future. Then the British government had been the sole arbiter of future development. But British policy had been tentative, and in the first half of the twentieth century the districts into which the Protectorate had been divided had developed a strong sense of separate identity, in many cases because district boundaries had coincided with tribal frontiers. In Toro this feeling may have been limited very largely to the rulers and their privileged supporters, but if the rest of the population had little feeling of loyalty for the kingdom, many had now become attached to the Mukama and few had any sense of identity with the other districts of which the Western Province was made up.

Between the wars the activities of the Legislative Council had made little impact upon the lives of the people of Toro. Its membership had been small and the unofficial representation had only risen from 2, both Europeans, in 1921, to 4 in 1933 when a second Asian was appointed. The first African members were admitted in 1945 and the then enlarged Western Province had been supposedly represented by the *katikkiros* of Bunyoro and Toro and the Nganzi of Ankole in turn. The nature of these appointments had made it clear that the attitude of the Protectorate authorities towards the Legislative Council had not changed. It was still to be, primarily, a consultative committee which provided the Administration with an opportunity to explain its policies to those whose cooperation it required. Needless to say, it was an arrangement which suited the Mukama of Toro reasonably well, for if African participation in the Legislative Council was now to be encouraged it was better that the members should be men of whom the rulers approved and whom they did, in fact, control. In any event the Legislative Council still appeared to have little relevance for Toro.

This paternalism on the part of the Protectorate Administration was breached minimally in 1949. After the reinstitution of the Northern Province it was agreed that each of the four provinces should be invited to send two representatives to the Council. In the case of the Western Province one of the two would be elected by the newly created Provincial Council while the other would be nominated in turn by the rulers of Bunyoro, Toro and Ankole. The narrowness of the breach was emphasized by the fact that the districts felt little association with the man supposedly elected to represent their interests. The next stage in the development of the influence of the Legislative Council had to wait a further four years.

In the meantime, Toro was being drawn steadily and unobtrusively into closer association with the Protectorate as a whole. The Protectorate authorities were becoming increasingly conscious of the fact that if the standards of living of the people of Uganda were to improve there must be a considerable increase in the country's wealth. The rise in prices in the later 1940s had given an exaggerated impression of the country's output and it was considered that the cotton industry, Uganda's main source of wealth, must be stimulated. A commission of enquiry reported in 1948 that buyers and ginners in many cases cheated the growers, while another commission reported adversely on the mechanical state of the country's ginneries. In 1949 the Administration attempted to stabilize the industry by setting up a Lint Marketing Board which would guarantee fair prices to growers and protect the quality of the cotton.

Another project which was to have repercussions in Toro was the creation of the Uganda Fish Marketing Board which was to purchase the hauls of the fishermen of Lake Edward and Lake George for marketing in Kampala and other centres of the Protectorate. In the early 1950s, too, the Protectorate Administration tried to develop Uganda's industrial potential by setting up a Uganda Development Corporation with an initial capital of £5 millions. The aim was to encourage development schemes by providing in some cases the sort of financial support which would attract private companies to invest in Uganda. For Toro, the most important outcome of this programme was the reopening of the Kilembe Copper Mines, on a much larger scale than ever before, as a joint enterprise in which Messrs. Frobisher Limited were associated with the Uganda Development Corporation and the Colonial Development Corporation. Following upon this came the western extension of the railway from Kampala to Kilembe, which linked Toro by rail with the Indian Ocean. All these developments meant more opportunities for employment and more wealth for the people of the kingdom and resulted in an increasing involvement in the affairs of Toro by Protectorate agents.

Yet, within its borders, the kingdom contrived to retain its identity. The administrative changes which took place in the early 1950s, however, presented a more direct challenge to the kingdom's individualism than the more insidious effects of economic development. In 1953 Sir Andrew Cohen, who had become Governor of Uganda in the previous year, took the first step towards converting the Legislative Council into a rudimentary parliament by increasing the unofficial membership and by attempting at the same time to make it more genuinely representative of the African population. Instead of being nominated by traditional rulers or elected by artificial provincial councils the African unofficial members, other than those from Buganda, were to be elected by district councils. The effect of this change was that elected members for the first time regarded themselves as representing a constituency, although it did not mean that they immediately thought of themselves as leading their constituencies into a closer association with the rest of the Protectorate. On the contrary, the districts became more consciously separatist. Because the British had introduced a version of the Buganda system of administration into the other parts of the Protectorate for reasons of economy, it had become the goal of every district to reproduce the near-autonomous position of Buganda and also the special relationship enjoyed by Buganda with the Protectorate Administration. In Toro especially, Kasagama and then Rukidi had cherished the hope that the 1900 Agreement might enable them to sample the privileges indulged in by Buganda as a result of the 1900 Buganda Agreement.

For Toro, then, the election of a member to sit in the Legislative Council seemed no more than the appointment of a delegate to represent the kingdom's views in the central deliberations of the Protectorate. The first member to be elected, Mr J. K. Babiiha, took his seat early in 1954 and defended Toro's interests wholeheartedly. Although he was in time to become deeply involved in the political life of the Protectorate as a whole he never ceased to keep in close touch with the Mukama.

Another figure from the western kingdom also found his way into the new Legislative Council. Mr T. B. Bazarrabuza was a Mukonjo, a former mission school teacher and schools inspector. He was, in the first instance, appointed by the Governor as a member of the experimental cross-bench, lightly referred to by representative members as Cohen's kindergarten, which consisted of individual Europeans, Asians and Africans chosen for their particular experience or personal qualities. The experiment was short-lived and Bazarrabuza, along with the other members of the cross-bench, found himself a government backbencher, free however to vote as he wished except over issues of confidence. Although he regarded himself as possessing a more general brief than did Babiiha, Toro's elected representative,

Bazarrabuza was nevertheless a loyal supporter of the Mukama and, possessing something of the same simple directness of character as did Rukidi himself, and an instinctive grasp of the needs of ordinary people, he pursued the interests of Toro within the wider framework of development offered by Uganda as a whole.

The strength of tradition, even if – as in the case of Toro – of a relatively recent origin, was to be similarly tested by the Administration's attempts to reform local government. In 1953 a report was published, prepared by Mr C. A. G. Wallis, which attempted to explain the character of local administration and its relationship with the central government. It stressed the danger of Uganda's developing into a federal rather than a unitary state and urged that chiefs should cease to be rulers, law-givers and representatives of the central government, and instead should become the agents of local authorities, executing the decisions of elected councils in matters of purely local concern.[6] These recommendations ran contrary to the trend of development over the previous fifty years in Uganda and were particularly disturbing to the Agreement districts of which Toro was one. Speaking in the Legislative Council when the District Councils Bill, which embodied Wallis's proposals, was debated, Babiiha stressed the importance attached by the Batoro to the role of the Mukama and urged that this be kept in mind. He also said that he hoped that the participation of elected representatives in the Legislative Council would not detract from the powers of the Mukama.[7] As a consequence of the doubts expressed by several of the members the Bill was enacted as an enabling ordinance rather than as a compulsory measure and Toro could relax once more.

Now were heard the first murmurs of an argument which was to grow in volume and in strength and ultimately to lead to the destruction of the kingdom. In 1952 the Uganda National Congress was founded. Its creators were Mr I. K. Musazi and Mr A. M. K. Mayanja, both Baganda, but it set out to be an interracial association and its aims included the unification of all the peoples of Uganda and the achievement of self-government on a basis of universal suffrage. Initially the movement got little support and for a time it was partially diverted from its main objectives when the Governor deposed and deported Kabaka Mutesa in 1953 for having allegedly broken the Buganda Agreement. The energies of the Congress, whose members were mainly Baganda, were then devoted to the task of bringing about the Kabaka's restoration, and although they maintained that self-government remained their aim their involvement with the affairs of Buganda weakened their impact upon Africans in the rest of the Protectorate. On Mutesa's return in 1955 one of the stipulations of the newly negotiated Buganda Agreement was that the kingdom should send representatives to the Legislative Council. Owing to the part they had played in bringing about the Kabaka's restoration, and as a tribute to their skill in political skirmishing, four out of five of the members sent to represent Buganda were Congress men, one of them being the co-founder, Musazi.

The influence of the Congress members in the Legislative Council was very quickly felt. Vigorous in debate, they attempted to assert their position as spokesmen for the African people of Uganda and to seize the political initiative by making demands for immediate constitutional reform. The representatives from the districts outside Buganda, who had been learning their craft as members of the Council under the skilled presidency of Sir Andrew Cohen for the past two years, strongly resented the efforts of the Congress members both to usurp the role they had themselves been developing inside the Council and their status as representatives of popular opinion outside the council chamber. To oppose the Congress members absolutely, however, was to appear as lackeys of the Protectorate Administration. The predicament of the non-Baganda members was illustrated by their reaction to Dr E. M. K. Muwazi's motion urging the Administration to consider sympathetically a proposal to introduce direct elections for all representative members in 1957.[8] The object of the motion was primarily to enable the Congress members to escape from their dependence upon the Buganda *Lukiiko*, which acted as an electoral college, but as an apparently democratic proposal it was one for which all representative members had some sympathy. The representative from Bunyoro, Mr G. B. K. Magezi, attempted a compromise by moving an amendment calling for the deletion of all reference to timing, but Babiiha considered that the only position open to him was to abstain when the motion was put to the vote.

Thus without conscious planning and in reaction to what seemed like the threat of Buganda domination, most of the African representatives in the Council found themselves aligned with the Governor in his campaign to encourage the growth of political awareness and to prepare for self-government within a unified state. This also implied support for an integrated scheme of economic growth, the extension of educational opportunities and a sound constitutional training inside the Legislative Council.

The shadow of Buganda continued to hang over the Protectorate, and not least over Toro, where the Mukama was carefully watching the reaction of the Protectorate Administration to the increasingly independent line of action pursued by the Kabaka's Government. Not only the Mukama's interest but that of many others in different parts of Uganda was aroused in April 1956 when Sir Andrew Cohen, responding to the debate on Dr Muwazi's motion, proposed the introduction of direct elections in Buganda in 1959 and in the rest of the Protectorate in 1961. The representative members of the Council from outside Buganda were opposed to the differentiation implied by the Governor's scheme, yet it was once again a Congress member, Dr B. N. Kununka, who seized the initiative. A constitutional committee was appointed to consider Cohen's proposal and, goaded into action by Kununka's skilled advocacy, the representative members sitting in the committee pressed for simultaneous constitutional advance throughout the Protectorate. A compromise was then reached which allowed for the direct election of all African representatives in 1958 and common roll elections in 1961 with a guarantee that there would be an adequate and effective representation of non-Africans.[9]

The Congress members still retained the initiative, but gradually the other African representative members began to hit back. Their opportunity came in April 1957 when a Congress member of Council introduced a motion calling for self-government in 1958 and unwisely referred to the discussions between the Protectorate Administration and representatives of Buganda which had preceded the Kabaka's return from exile. At once the non-Baganda members pounced. Magezi was the first to speak. Condemning the discussions on the grounds that they had affected the whole Protectorate without any reference to the opinion of other districts, he argued that the Congress members were closely linked with Baganda interests and did not represent the rest of Uganda. Babiiha followed, accusing Mr Y. S. Bamuta, the mover of the motion, of having failed to consult the non-Baganda members before introducing the subject into the Council. He also criticized the Congress members for attempting to incite the people against their true representatives and, pouring scorn upon the precipitate character of Bamuta's proposal, asked pointedly what would become of the rulers of the kingdoms under immediate self-government. The Bakama, he said, thought of their kingdoms as national entities, with the inhabitants as their subjects and themselves as responsible to the British Government, and he asked how they could possibly be accommodated within Bamuta's scheme.[10] Babiiha's ambivalent role as defender of the ancient rights of Toro and a democratically elected member of the central legislature was clearly in evidence.

Bamuta's motion was lost, but the demand for self-government was gaining momentum. However, the problem of integrating the kingdoms into a self-governing Uganda was very far from being resolved. The representatives of the kingdoms were in a difficult position for they were, at the same time, attempting to protect the interests and identity of their states within a state while being drawn together with the other districts of Uganda to resist the overweening claims of Buganda. In the debate on direct elections which took place in August 1967 Babiiha found himself drawing attention to a resolution passed by the Buganda *Lukiiko* which called for a federal Uganda under the leadership of the Kabaka of Buganda.[11] Later in the year he pursued a similar theme in the debate on the Administration's motion to approve the introduction in 1961 of direct elections for representative members on a common roll with safeguards for racial minorities. He was deeply concerned at the way in which Buganda always seemed to be given a head start over the rest of the Protectorate and at the particular attention paid by the Colonial Office to Buganda opinion while neglecting the other districts,[12] a concern which appeared to be justified when the Colonial Secretary refused to meet a delegation of representative members in March and again in June 1958. In these circumstances the valedictory message of Governor Sir Frederick Crawford on the dissolution of the Legislative Council at the end of its term of office in 1958 had a hollow ring when he described the Council as 'a democratic parliamentary institution for the Protectorate as a whole'.[13]

The description nevertheless indicated a profound change in the attitude of the Protectorate authorities towards the Legislative Council since 1945, but the non-Baganda members doubted the sincerity of this conversion. When the new Council assembled later in 1958 the direct elections had resulted in the return of Babiiha and most of the other non-Baganda members of the former Council, but Buganda had simply refused to hold elections of any sort, and shortly afterwards, in consequence of a constitutional quibble, Buganda withdrew even its nominated representatives. The gap between the interests of Buganda and the rest of the country was becoming wider and the majority of the African members of the Council decided to form themselves into a party which, unlike the Congress, would be based outside Buganda.[14] The members of the new party, the Uganda Peoples Union, were, however, more concerned with the development of parliamentary institutions than with creating a nationwide party organization, and the U.P.U. retained more of the character of a parliamentary party than of a popular movement. This was a reflection of the members' view that they represented districts rather than the Protectorate as a whole, and that their joint action was occasioned less by the need to present a common African front to the Protectorate Administration than to defend their individual interests against the power of Buganda.

The voice of Buganda was becoming increasingly strident and it was not now the members of the Congress who were calling the tune but the kingdom's more conservative leaders, whose aim was to protect the traditional powers of the Buganda hierarchy rather than to promote the democratic process. Again, the representatives of the other districts found themselves almost unconsciously adopting the cause of democracy in order to meet Buganda's challenge. This tendency became still more pronounced after the appointment of a committee in February 1959 under the chairmanship of the administrative secretary, Mr J. V. Wild, to make recommendations regarding the common roll elections in 1961. Although most districts greeted the committee with enthusiasm, Buganda, with the exception of a few courageous individuals, remained firmly aloof. There were several members of the committee as well as of the Legislative Council who would have rejoiced to see the Protectorate Administration take the Buganda Government to task for flouting its obligations to the Protectorate as whole and to the new Buganda Agreement. But in April 1959 news reached Uganda that the Colonial Secretary had stated that there was no intention of putting an end to the Agreement in spite of Buganda's request that it should be terminated.

It was at this moment that several elect members of the Legislative Council came to the conclusion that they must carry the struggle against Buganda outside the Council. If the Protectorate Administration would not respond to pressure from the elected representatives of the people, then the people must form themselves into an effective political association to present their case. Thus another stage was reached in the country's constitutional development, and the Toro monarchy found itself in the strange position of being apparently defended by a popular movement which was demanding greater democracy in Uganda as a whole.

This paradox was reflected in the memorandum submitted by Mr Babiiha to the Wild Committee. In it he attempted to set out a compromise solution, avoiding the extremes of unitary government on the one hand and federal government on the other. The proposals were not wholly clear, but the goal appeared to be a form of constitutional monarchy in which there would be a Council of State consisting of the rulers of the kingdoms, each of whom would serve in turn as head of state for a period of five years during the life of one parliament. There would be a bicameral legislature, with a senate and a house of representatives, and day-to-day government would be carried on by the political party which gained a majority as a result of common roll elections.

That the scheme had the approval of the Mukama of Toro there can be no doubt. Rukidi was shrewdly aware of the many pressures making for constitutional change in the Protectorate and Babiiha's proposals, even if difficult to implement, had emphasized the need to respect the monarchs even in an independent Uganda, and at the same time they ensured the preservation of the kingdoms. The members of the Wild Committee, however, were more immediately concerned with avoiding a situation in which Buganda, in an attempt to preserve its traditions, might break away from the rest of the Protectorate. Their report, therefore, emphasized the need to introduce a unitary form of government for a self-governing and ultimately independent Uganda and concerned itself with the rulers only to the extent of ensuring that their dignity was preserved.[15]

The confidence of the traditional Baganda leaders was shaken by the unanimity of the report and the bold recommendations which it contained. For a brief period it seemed that the dominant voice which Buganda had had in the constitutional affairs of the Protectorate would be muted. The Colonial Office, however, beset by world-wide problems, hesitated to take up the challenge thrown down by the Wild Committee and the Baganda regained their composure. Many of the non-Baganda members of the Legislative Council had taken part in the Wild Committee, where their efforts had been concentrated upon producing a workable constitutional scheme. Now they realized that their dialogue with the Protectorate Administration had gone as far as it could in the limited form which the proceedings of the Legislative Council made possible. If they were to make further progress it must be on the basis of popular political agitation.

With the exception of Mr A. M. Obote, the member from Lango District who had been a member of the Congress, few of them were party men. As the report was taking shape, however, they had come to recognize that its implementation would depend heavily upon an effective party structure throughout the country. The British Government's cautious reaction to their recommendations and the revival of the spirits of the Baganda leaders encouraged an amalgamation between the Uganda Peoples Union, whose members had hitherto shown their abilities mainly within the Legislative Council, and Obote's branch of the Congress, to form the Uganda Peoples Congress. The new party had little support in Buganda, where the only active political party – and that a numerically weak one – was the Democratic Party, many of whose leaders were Roman Catholics who, owing to the vagaries of Buganda's constitutional history, had little hope of achieving power within the traditional framework of the kingdom. Against both parties there loomed the power of the Buganda monarchy and its supporters.

Uganda was on the road to independence but its constitutional future now seemed to depend almost entirely upon the outcome of the struggle between the traditionalist Baganda and the newly mustered forces of democracy in the rest of the country. It was time for Rukidi to review the role of his own small kingdom when the giants joined battle.

VI · The Kingdom Again Destroyed

The period between the publication of the Wild Committee's Report and Uganda's achievement of independence was one of constitutional confusion. Only one group, the supporters of the Buganda monarchy, pursued a consistent aim and even they resorted to methods which at times appeared to reverse their earlier tactics. Rukidi and his followers, anxious to maintain the Kingdom of Toro intact, were torn between a policy of attempting to achieve their goal by emulating Buganda's secessionist inclinations and one of cooperating more closely with the Protectorate authorities in the move to achieve a unitary state. The prospect of working with Buganda was not one which could fill the Mukama with confidence. The extent of Buganda's claims was unpredictable and might not always be beneficial to her allies. In 1958 she had even implied in a document to the British Government that Toro, Ankole and Bunyoro had formerly been dependencies of Buganda.[1] On the other hand, in spite of a declaration by the Governor in February 1960 that measures would be taken to protect the dignity and status of the rulers, and in spite also of the financial advantages likely to accrue from a close association with the rest of Uganda, there was no denying the fact that a democratically ruled society was totally at variance with the Toro founded by Kaboyo and fostered by Kasagama.

In an attempt to bridge the gap between separate action by the kingdoms and their complete absorption in a unitary Uganda, Rukidi joined with the Kabaka of Buganda and the Mugabe of Ankole to issue what was referred to as the 'Rulers' Proclamation' on 20 February 1960. This document called for a meeting of *katikkiros* to discuss ways and means of safeguarding the right of the people of the kingdoms to choose and change their own form of government. It was an important step, for out of the meetings which followed came the proposal that Uganda should develop as a federal state. Neither Bunyoro, which supported the move although the Mukama, due to a long-felt distrust of Buganda did not sign the proclamation, nor Ankole, was quite so firmly wedded to the federal scheme as were Buganda and Toro, nor were the two latter kingdoms ever very explicit about their interpretation of federalism. But the opposition to the traditional British view that Uganda would develop as a unitary state was sufficiently strong to induce the British Government to send a commission to Uganda to make recommendations regarding the future form of government and in particular regarding the relations between the central government of Uganda and the other authorities in the country, notably the governments of the kingdoms which had agreements with Britain. Elections on the basis of the Wild Committee's recommendations would, however, take place before the commission reported, and the report would then be followed by a constitutional conference at which the kingdoms, as well as the new, democratically chosen legislature, would be represented.

Meanwhile the task of cooperating with Buganda on a consistent basis was proving difficult. Throughout 1960 and while the *katikkiros* were holding discussions with the leaders of the other local governments, the *Lukiiko* continued to press for the termination of the agreements between Buganda and Britain so that the kingdom could make its own terms with its neighbours when independence was achieved. Various members of the Legislative Council, representatives of the western kingdoms prominent among them, urged the Protectorate Administration not to give Buganda special treatment,[2] but Buganda ignored their protests. The British Government having rejected a demand that the Commission should report before the elections or else that Buganda should be guaranteed federal status, the kingdom declared its unilateral independence on 1 January 1961.

The immediate constitutional effects of this action were negligible. The Protectorate Administration refused to recognize the independence of the kingdom and day-to-day government continued unaffected. The most important result was that when the Relationships Commission, under the chairmanship of Lord Munster, arrived in the Protectorate in January, the Buganda question immediately occupied the centre of their considerations. 'It is hardly too much to say that every serious problem which we encountered in Uganda had its roots in the Buganda problem', they wrote.[3] Toro, they said, though so much smaller, had had its appetite for autonomy whetted by the example of Buganda, and Buganda's disregard of the authority of the Protectorate Administration had strengthened Toro's resistance to local government reform.[4] This degree of association between the two kingdoms was the most that the Commission would admit. Although insisting that Buganda had a vital role to play in an independent Uganda and that secession was unacceptable they were prepared to recommend federal status for the kingdom. For the other kingdoms, however, on grounds of their smallness and of the nature of their historical relationship with Britain, they suggested only a semi-federal relationship which, while protecting the status of the rulers, the succession, royal ceremonial and local customs, would leave them in all other respects in the same position as the non-Agreement districts.[5]

Even while the Commission was considering its report the Buganda hierarchy had again shown its strength. In August 1960 registration had taken place for the elections to be held in the following year and, owing to pressure from the Buganda Government, only 35,000 people registered in the kingdom out of an estimated 700,000 who were qualified. When the elections took place in 1961 even fewer went to the polls, with the result that the Democratic Party, with a handful of votes, won twenty out of twenty-one seats in Buganda, and this enabled it to gain a majority over its rival, the U.P.C. A government was formed with Mr Benedicto Kiwanuka, leader of the D.P., as leader of the Legislative Council, supported by ten D.P. ministers.

The situation was a complicated one. The victorious party had virtually no experience of working in the Legislative Council, all the long-term members being on the opposition benches. This was a triumph for Buganda, however, for the U.P.C. had been the chief critics of Buganda's policy and the main protagonists of a unitary state. The Democratic Party was not such a formidable machine, and although some of its leaders were men of quality they depended too heavily upon their Buganda seats for their own peace of mind, especially when the Buganda hierarchy turned its attack upon them, as it quickly did. The success of the boycott on registration had given some idea of the hostility of the Buganda Government to a party whose very name challenged the traditional Buganda system. Moreover, so strong was the loyalty of the Baganda to their ruler that it was only necessary to draw their attention to the impossibility of accepting a Muganda commoner, Kiwanuka, in a role which placed him above the Kabaka, to destroy any hopes he may have had of successfully controlling Uganda's affairs. Buganda held all the cards.

The leader of the U.P.C., Milton Obote, a shrewd politician, had for some years been assessing the problem of Buganda's relations with the rest of the country and had noticeably refrained from attacking the kingdom as vigorously as had many of his colleagues. Sensing the difficulties which would lie ahead if he continued in conflict with Buganda he now determined to work for cooperation with the leaders of the kingdom. It was a surprising move, yet the only possible one if Uganda was not to disintegrate and if the U.P.C. was to form a workable government in the future. At the conference which opened in London on 18 September 1961 to work out a constitution for an internally self-governing Uganda, Obote therefore supported

Buganda's claim to use the *Lukiiko* as an electoral college for selecting Buganda's representatives to the legislature. Kiwanuka could not accept this if his Democratic Party was to survive in Buganda, although even direct elections would have been of little use to him if the Buganda Government had put up candidates against his party. He was in a cleft stick and Obote had out-manoeuvred him. Yet Obote was by no means in command of the situation. He badly needed Buganda's cooperation, but if he made too many concessions to the Kabaka's Government the rest of Uganda, from which his party drew its strength, would believe he had betrayed their interests. The U.P.C. therefore submitted a memorandum to the Colonial Secretary rejecting the term semi-federal as applied by the Munster Commission to the other kingdoms and urged that they be granted federal status without, however, making any great concessions. Again Kiwanuka had been out-generalled, and although he became the country's first Prime Minister when Uganda achieved internal self-government on 1 March 1962 his position was weak. With an election pending and an alliance, even if only of expediency, between the U.P.C. and the Kabaka's Government, his future was insecure.

While Buganda held the limelight in the negotiations with the British Government the Toro Government had been watching carefully and learning rapidly. Rukidi had envied the strong position occupied by the Kabaka as a constitutional ruler since the 1955 Buganda Agreement. In 1961, therefore, negotiations took place between representatives of Toro and the Protectorate Administration with a view to drafting a new Agreement which would permit Britain, in advance of the pre-independence constitutional conference, to protect the Mukama and to guarantee a ministerial form of government for Toro within an independent Uganda. The British authorities argued that any agreement could only be of a provisional nature because the country was on the verge of independence when all agreements between Britain and the component parts of Uganda would be terminated. To have any lasting effect its terms must be embodied in Uganda's independence constitution. The Mukama, however, pressed his point because he believed that only on the basis of a new agreement could he successfully insist upon the federal status for Toro which was now his aim.

Enlisting the aid of Mr Dingle Foot Q.C., Rukidi pursued his demands through the agency of a constitutional committee which he empowered to discuss federal status with the Governor, and early in 1962 Foot stated on behalf of Toro that unless a more satisfactory constitutional arrangement could be reached by the time British protection was withdrawn the kingdom would revert to its former independence. This threat was an echo of the argument frequently put forward by the Baganda leaders who claimed that, because Buganda had made agreements with Britain only, the termination of the agreements would automatically sever the links between the kingdom and the rest of the Protectorate which Britain had instituted purely for administrative convenience. Toro's threat, however, carried far less weight with Britain than did those of Buganda, and the constitutional discussion having reached stalemate, the Toro Government was reduced to making its disapproval felt by the insignificant gesture of refusing to arrange celebrations in recognition of Uganda's achievement of internal self-government on 1 March.

Support for Toro's pretensions came from an unexpected quarter, but to little purpose. In March 1962 the Democratic Party decided that in order to counter the challenge of the U.P.C./Buganda alliance it must seek support on a wider front, and so belatedly announced its approval of federal status for the other kingdoms. This, in itself, was a serious reversal of the party's policy for it had claimed for almost a year that it was the only group which really desired a democratic form of government in Uganda, and Kiwanuka took even this step with less than minimum skill. Attempting to put himself in the forefront of the campaign for federal status he pressed for the postponement of the pre-independence elections to the National Assembly until his wishes had been granted, and by so doing he laid himself open to the charge of trying unfairly to prolong the life of his own government. Not content with this tactical error he proceeded to make another false move by threatening that Uganda might have to leave the Commonwealth in order to achieve a federal form of government.[6] The Democratic Party's credibility as leader of a united Uganda was thus destroyed by the obduracy of the kingdoms and the inexperience of its leaders.

Yet the U.P.C. was uneasy. As the memorandum presented to the Colonial Secretary in September 1961 had implied, the Congress did not consider that to confer federal status upon the kingdoms would involve any significant transfer of powers, for that would have meant an undue weakening of the Central Government which they themselves hoped to control in the near future. But the U.P.C. representatives from the kingdoms found themselves with divided loyalties when the terms of the Local Administrations Bill, which became law in February 1962, were made known, and it was seen that the powers devolving upon the western kingdoms were scarcely larger than those to be exercised by the other districts. This was far less than had been anticipated when negotiations had taken place in 1961 for the Toro Provisional Agreement, and Toro was deeply dissatisfied with the Bill. John Babiiha criticized it vigorously in the course of the debate in the Legislative Council, but to no avail. So strong was popular feeling in the kingdom, however, that both the U.P.C. and the D.P. candidates refused to register for the elections to the National Assembly in protest against the Bill.

At that moment the fundamental weakness of the U.P.C. stood revealed. It was not a truly national party. Other considerations apart, it was impossible for the party's leaders to conduct an election campaign throughout the country because of the wide range of languages spoken in the different districts.

Obote, for example, could only speak in Toro through an interpreter, unless he addressed his remarks to the relatively few who understood English. Consequently, any political party relied for its support upon the backing its individual members could command in their own districts, rather than upon popular approval of a national policy. But where local loyalties were as strong as they were in Toro even such a committed party man as Babiiha was bound to find himself in difficulties when U.P.C. policies appeared to conflict with Toro's interests.

In these circumstances a federal system may have seemed the only answer to the problem, but the Toro leaders were unable to seize the opportunity offered by the disarray of the two main political parties. In the first place they were unsure of their tactics. More mature consideration had suggested that their threat to proclaim the kingdom's independence was unrealistic and they now fell back upon the less spectacular but equally impractical alternative of demanding the continuation of British protection if federal status were not approved.[7] A second problem had now also arisen and this was one which was to bedevil the kingdom for several years. The leaders who had made such play with the importance of the agreements, both in their negotiations with the British authorities and in preparing the way for independence, now found themselves having the system used against them, and by unexpected assailants.

Although Rukidi's personal popularity had won him the adherence of counties which had felt only lukewarm towards his father, the Toro hierarchy had continued to treat the Baamba and the Bakonjo with something like contempt. In March 1962 the seventeen Baamba and Bakonjo members walked out of a meeting of the *Rukurato* in support of their claim for the creation of a separate district, and in a letter to the *Uganda Argus* of 9 April a correspondent, signing himself H. Mwamba, claimed that Bwamba had never been part of Toro and challenged the Toro Government to produce any agreement by which Bwanba had accepted the sovereignty of the Mukama of Toro.

Although the British Government acceded to the reiterated demand for federal status for the western kingdoms only a few days later, the Mukama was in no mood to agree to the secession of part of Toro. For the moment, however, he was less concerned about refractory elements in his own kingdom than with protecting Toro against external pressures in the closing weeks of the negotiations leading up to independence. His fears were roused when, after Toro had complained that Buganda had not congratulated her upon achieving federal status, the Buganda information officer contemptuously replied that the western kingdoms had not been given federal status but had been fooled by the politicians. Toro's vacillation had already resulted in a delay in the holding of elections to the National Assembly, except in the constituencies of Bwamba and Busongora, and when they did take place distrust of Buganda, and of the U.P.C.'s alliance with the Kabaka's supporters, induced the other constituencies to follow the lead already given by Bwamba and Busongora by returning Democratic Party candidates. Hitherto the kingdom had been represented by members of the U.P.C. and this reversal demonstrated clearly the uncertainty of the Toro leadership as to how it should protect its authority.

In spite of defections in the western kingdoms the U.P.C./Buganda alliance won a great victory in the elections and it was Obote who led the Uganda Government delegation to the final constitutional conference in London in June 1962. Even then his main worry arose from the continuing demands of the kingdoms, which threatened to split any vestige of unity which Uganda might hope to preserve. The Mukama of Toro, present in London for the conference, announced that he would insist upon the existing agreement remaining in force until a new one accepting Toro's claims had been signed, and for a time the Toro representatives boycotted the conference. In conjunction with the other western kingdoms the Toro leaders then insisted upon protecting their position by entering into short-term agreements with Britain on the understanding that with British help the agreements would be incorporated in the independence constitution, as in the event they were. The main provisions of the agreements included the determination of the royal succession, which was to be the prerogative of the ruler, though if he failed to carry out his obligation it would devolve upon specified senior officials of the kingdom, the Uganda Parliament having no say in the matter. Each kingdom was also to have a Council of Ministers and a legislature with limited powers, and a Public Service Commission.

These apparently generous concessions induced the kingdoms to accept the constitution, but when the Administrations (Western Kingdoms and Busoga) Bill was introduced into Parliament to make the provisions effective there was sharp criticism of the excessive control reserved to the Minister of Regional Administration and a new draft had to be prepared. Even then the kingdoms were still seen to have their powers greatly restricted. Any laws which the legislatures of the kingdoms enacted under the authority delegated by the Central Government, as opposed to those areas of legislation authorized by the constitution, required the approval of the Minister for Regional Administration. Where the duties of chiefs as agents of the Central Government conflicted with their obligations to the Kingdom Government, the former took precedence. Parliament it was, too, which laid down the taxes that a kingdom might levy, and it retained the right to determine the conditions under which any payment was made by the Central Government to the local authority. Thus the powers of the kingdoms differed only minimally from those of the other districts, although up to a point they were guaranteed by the constitution. To that extent the ruler's insistence upon the signing of prior agreements with the British Government had proved of benefit.

More fundamentally, however, the Mukama of Toro was in a weaker position than Kasagama had been after the signing of the 1900 Agreement, for in 1900 the Central Government, that is the Protectorate Administration, had only limited plans for the development of Uganda, and interference in Toro's affairs was likely to be slight, provided peace and order were maintained. By contrast in 1962, and in spite of Toro's federal status, the Central Government's development programmes envisaged a considerable amount of control throughout the whole of Uganda, except in Buganda. Rukidi might well have accepted this situation, for his long-drawn-out fight for federal status had sprung from his desire to retain a strong personal authority over his people rather than from any hostility towards the sort of economic development which called for countrywide organization, or from any wish to participate in the formulation of Uganda's external policy. Indeed, his opposition to the Administrations (Western Kingdoms) Act had been directed less against specific clauses than against the general concept of excessive interference by the Central Government in Toro's by now traditional way of doing things. It was unfortunate, therefore, that the discontent of the Baamba and Bakonjo, a matter which he regarded as falling solely within his own jurisdiction, should have led almost at once to the intervention of the central authority.

In August 1962 the leaders of the Baamba-Bakonjo movement threatened to go over the head of the Mukama by presenting a memorandum to the Minister of Regional Administration asking for secession from Toro. The Acting Prime Minister, Mr George Magezi, announced in September that a Commission of Inquiry into the situation in Bwamba would not begin its work until the disturbances which were now spreading through the area had been brought to an end. The leaders of the Baamba replied that there could be no peace until secession had been agreed, but to avoid deadlock the investigation went forward. The Commission rejected the idea of secession but maintained that the Toro Government was largely responsible for the recent unrest and that until the Batoro ceased to regard their Baamba and Bakonjo neighbours as less than human there could be no satisfactory solution. It was essential that the Baamba and the Bakonjo should have fair representation on all committees in the kingdom and that there should be better educational provision in the troubled areas.

The strong Democratic Party element in the Commission led to claims that the party was unduly sympathetic to the dissident elements in the kingdom and might even be implicated in the disturbances. This was strongly denied by the D.P. leaders and was almost certainly no more than a reflection of the Toro Government's resentment at being criticized by people from outside the kingdom. The Government's reluctance to comment officially upon the report, however, only aroused further distrust and in January 1963 both Bwamba and Busongora were declared disturbed areas. The Rwenzururu movement, as the secessionists now called themselves, was involved in armed struggles with police and a group under the leadership of Isaya Mukirane, a Mukonjo and a former school teacher, kidnapped a member of parliament, Mr Erizani Bwambale, but he was released shortly afterwards.

Under continuing pressure from the Uganda Rifles many Baamba and Bakonjo fled across the border into the Congo. This led to a protest from the Congo Government. After mediation by a British journalist, Mr Tom Stacey, who was known to many of the Bakonjo leaders, including Mukirane, the Uganda Government agreed to appoint a further Commission of Inquiry into the administration of the counties of Bwamba, Busongora, Burahya and Bunyangabo by the Toro authorities. The Toro Government responded in traditional fashion. Samson Rusoke who, true to the Toro pattern of keeping high office in a small number of leading families, held the appointment of *katikkiro* – or *muhikirawa* as it was now called – which his father had previously occupied, complained that the Mukama's Government had not been notified in advance that a commission was to be appointed. His protest carried less weight with the new Uganda Government than it would have done with the former

Protectorate Administration. In March 1963 the Government issued a White Paper on Toro accepting the recommendation of the Commission which had carried out investigations in the previous year that there should be no secession and that the Toro Government, if not wholly blameless, was not entirely responsible for the disturbances which had taken place. However, the Government insisted that for the time being Bakonjo and Baamba chiefs should be appointed to serve in their own counties, and that if strong county councils were not set up by the Mukama in the disturbed areas the Central Government would do so itself. Measures must also be taken to redress the grievances of the Bakonjo and the Baamba. Doubtless Rukidi looked back regretfully to the days of the more complaisant Stephen Bagge, who had simply told protestors that the Mukama was the supreme authority.

A month later, in April, the Central Government decided to take control of education and road-making in Bwamba and Busongora and appointed a British official to collect the Toro graduated tax in those counties because of the inefficiency of the Toro Government. Again a Toro deputation led by Samson Rusoke protested to the Central Government that the proposals would only lead to more trouble, but their comments made little impression upon their hearers. Shortly afterwards Rusoke encountered opposition to this authority in Toro itself when a vote of no confidence, which he believed to have been engineered by the Democratic Party acting in conjunction with dissident elements within the kingdom, was defeated in the *Rukurato* by only 26 votes to 24.

The disturbances in the kingdom had a variety of causes. The arrogance of the Toro Government towards the districts of Bwamba and Busongora has already been referred to. But the fact that protest now found a voice was due both to the spread of education, which encouraged people to question an authority they may formerly have resented but had not dared to criticize, and to the emergence of political parties which, however incompetently and however inconsistently, were endeavouring to impose an overall pattern upon Uganda and had stimulated a demand for a more democratic form of administration; even in the mountain regions of Ruwenzori. Both these factors, as well as the impression made by Tom Stacey's arguments, were reflected in a request from some of the better educated leaders of the Rwenzururu movement that the Uganda Government should endeavour to capture Isaya Mukirane who had become a nuisance by prolonging the disorder in Bwamba and Busongora, and in their appreciation of the improvements brought about the Central Government's intervention in the administration of the two countries. They stressed, however, that the need to establish a separate district still remained, and would continue to be the goal of their endeavours.[8]

Gratified though the Government may have been by this praise they had no desire to harry the Mukama of Toro further, and various ministers stressed that secession was not contemplated for either Bwamba or Busongora. Nor had the Government the means or the expertise to conduct an effective campaign against rebel elements in the mountainous country of Toro. Violence therefore became steadily more commonplace in spite of the vigorous efforts of security forces. In October 1964 the county headquarters of Bwamba was attacked by a large group of Rwenzururu supporters, and three months later Samson Rusoke announced that arrangements for the elections for the *Rukurato* had been delayed because of unrest.

In December 1965 Toro suffered a great loss when Rukidi died after ruling for thirty-seven years. He had struggled to maintain the kingdom which he had inherited from his father and, until the recent troubles, had been more than successful in his efforts. He had won the respect and the affection of many of his own subjects who were not particularly wedded to the idea of Toro overlordship, and also of many British officials. He had exercised considerable influence over the Kabaka of Buganda who had frequently looked to him for advice and encouragement during the difficulties he had encountered in his reign. Although a sturdy fighter for the rights of the Toro monarchy, Rukidi had been very conscious of the changes which must occur as the twentieth century unfolded. He had given way where to give way seemed to him beneficial to his kingdom, and he had resisted when he believed his rights were in danger. He had not always been master of events in his dealings either with the British Government or its agent, the Protectorate Administration, and still less so when he had had to negotiate with the Government of an independent Uganda. Perhaps his difficulty lay in the fact that his interest and his heart were in Toro, and because he saw all that was going on in the light of its immediate effect upon the kingdom he was unable to grasp some of the broader issues sufficiently firmly to recognize the true interests of Toro, even of his own Toro.

Had he lived on, Rukidi could not have defended the old-style monarchy against the advancing tide of Central Government interference, although the disaster which was to overthrow the old monarchy was not of Toro's immediate making. Rukidi's successor, Patrick, was also named Kaboyo, and with some prescience Rukidi had remarked not long before that Kaboyo had been the first of the kings of Toro and Patrick Kaboyo might well be the last. Yet the young Mukama, who was crowned in March 1966, could well have been the man to lead Toro into the new age. He was well educated and far from hostile to the aspirations of the Uganda Government. He recognized the difficulties which arose from the separatist tendencies of the different districts and was prepared to work for close cooperation with the central authorities. But, while Toro had been concerned with its Rwenzururu movement, deeper divisions had occurred outside the kingdom, and again Buganda had become the focus of attention.

In 1963 an opportunity had arisen to strengthen the tenuous bonds which joined the Buganda hierarchy to the U.P.C. It was agreed that the office of Governor-General, occupied since independence by Sir Walter Coutts, should be abolished and that a President should be appointed to be head of state in place of Queen Elizabeth II. Opinions differed as to who should hold the new office, but eventually Kabaka Mutesa was elected by Parliament. The pride of the Baganda was temporarily satisfied, but not for long. Independence had left one unsolved problem which the Baganda could not allow to be settled to their disadvantage. 'The Lost Counties' was a term applied by Bunyoro to a considerable area of territory acquired by the Baganda in the 1890s, at Bunyoro's expense, when Buganda was in an expansive mood and Britain had joined in to destroy the power of Kabarega. The whole or parts of seven counties were involved, but although Bunyoro consistently demanded the return of all seven, attention was mainly concentrated upon the counties of Buyaga and Bugangaizi. Not only were the inhabitants of those two counties still predominantly Banyoro, but Buyaga and Bugangaizi had for generations been at the heart of the Empire of Bunyoro-Kitara. The bones of many of the Bakama had been laid to rest there, and by special arrangement with Buganda guardians had been permitted to reside near the burial places to keep them in good order.[9]

With the approach of independence the Mukama of Bunyoro had pressed once again for the return of the Lost Counties, and early in 1962 the British Government appointed a commission under the chairmanship of Lord Molson to enquire into the case. The Commission rapidly concluded that a legal or even a historical approach would be unfruitful. The issue was confused by powerful personal feelings. Eventually a compromise solution was proposed under which Buganda was asked to hand back Buyaga and Bugangaizi while retaining control of the remaining territory.

The Kabaka rejected the plan and the Lost Counties became one of the main areas of contention at the pre-independence constitutional conference in June 1962. The Colonial Secretary, Reginald Maudling, tried to temporize by suggesting that the two counties should be administered by the Central Government for a two-year period at least, after which a referendum should be held to allow the inhabitants to decide where their allegiance should lie in the future. Obote accepted the proposal although he deplored the use of the term 'Lost Counties' because they still remained within Uganda and the usage only emphasized the divisions with which the country was beset. Buganda, however, rejected the scheme, and Bunyoro, too, remained critical on the surface, still hoping for the return of all the lost territory. Nevertheless, the arrangement was incorporated in the independence agreement and, sensing Obote's determination to carry out the referendum, the Kabaka spent as much time as he could in the 'Lost Counties' and even launched an ex-soldiers' settlement scheme there in order to increase the number of Baganda residents before a vote was taken. Obote, however, was too clever for him and insisted that the referendum should be based upon the pre-independence electoral roll. Although the Baganda challenged his ruling in the courts, the Prime Minister's decision was upheld and when the referendum took place in 1964 a large majority voted for a return to Bunyoro. The transfer of the administration was effected on 1 January 1965, to the great anger of the Baganda.

From that time the attitude of many Baganda towards Obote changed from dislike or contempt to outright hatred. He had flouted the wishes of their ruler and dragged the pride of the kingdom in the dust. There could be no further compromise. The struggle for power was now fully joined. The Buganda hierarchy must either triumph or be destroyed. Obote in his turn became increasingly arbitrary in his dealings with those around him and in February 1966 ordered the arrest of five members of his own cabinet, among them some of his oldest and staunchest supporters – notably from the western kingdoms – on charges of plotting against him and sympathizing with the Baganda. He then suspended the constitution and in April presented a new constitution to Parliament under which he himself became President and the entrenched privileges of the Baganda were abrogated.

The Buganda Government rejected the new proposals and ordered all Uganda Government troops to leave the kingdom by 30 May. Obote's forces then attacked the Kabaka's palace and although Mutesa made good his escape and after many adventures arrived in England, violent feelings had been aroused by the clash and the loss of life to which it had led. Obote attempted feebly to sort out the problem by restoring the Kingdom of Buganda on a more limited basis and urging the *Lukiiko* to elect a new Kabaka. From his place of exile, however, Mutesa announced that he was still the only true ruler of Buganda and his subjects fervently echoed his claim. Plots against Obote's Government proliferated and the President responded with greater repression.

In June 1967 another new constitution was presented to Parliament under which Uganda was to become a republic. Hitherto any attempt to define the nature of the constitution had been avoided by the use of the vague expression 'a federal parliamentary state'. This tribute to the strength of monarchical feeling in much of the country had even survived the appointment of a President. Now, however, Obote had reached the conclusion that for Buganda to continue in existence would be an insuperable obstacle to the successful government of Uganda. The kingdom was not only to be abolished; it was also to be dismembered – divided into districts which would be administered like the other districts in the republic. In its downfall, however, Buganda took with it the other kingdoms, including Toro. Their fate had been partly foreshadowed in a speech by the President in Kabale in April when he had criticized the rulers for preventing the inhabitants of the kingdoms from having a direct say in the country's affairs. 'Is it seriously suggested', he said, 'that in a united Uganda the rulers should continue to address the people of Uganda as "My people of Toro", "My people of Ankole", "My people of Buganda", "My people of

Bunyoro"?' The rulers, he went on, were responsible to no one, they did not have to explain their policies, they did not depend upon votes. This was an impossible situation.[10]

Yet Buganda was still Obote's main target. In spite of his conviction that some of his erstwhile supporters in the western kingdoms had betrayed him by sympathizing with Buganda he had no strong feelings against Toro, Bunyoro and Ankole, and Mukama Patrick Kaboyo had reaffirmed his support for the Central Government and stressed that the national interest must take precedence over local ambitions.[11] The decision to abolish the western kingdoms, therefore, was little more than the corollary to the proclamation of a republic. In this casual fashion a commoner from outside Toro had combined with a commoner within the kingdom, John Babiiha, now Vice-President, to destroy the monarchy, thus displaying what the traditionalists could only regard as contempt for what they now firmly believed to be ancient institutions, and so once again giving currency to the term *emigayo*.

The kingdom of Kaboyo, Nyaika, Kasagama and Rukidi was no more. They had created it and they had sustained it as the manifestation of their personal authority – an authority based upon ancient traditions, if not of Toro, then certainly of Bunyoro. Unlike Bunyoro, Toro had survived the first impact of British administration because Kasagama had not followed the lead given by Kabarega when he had resisted the British to the last, but had instead cooperated with the new rulers in their desire to impose an orderly system of administration. But if the British had used Kasagama he had made use of them, and had created the myth of an ancient and fairly extensive kingdom in which the British came to believe almost as fervently as he did himself. Alone he could have achieved little. With the loyal support of the Church Missionary Society's untiring agents and the complaisant acquiescence of the Protectorate Administration, he recreated in miniature much of the former glory of the Empire of Bunyoro-Kitara. It is true that the British imposed rigid territorial limits upon his aspirations, and in the west this had proved irksome. But in the north, the east and the south there were compensations. For if Toro could not expand in those directions the borders of the kingdom were secured by the Protectorate Administration from intrusion by rapacious Baganda monarchs, or by forces of retribution from Bunyoro.

The reign of Rukidi had shown that Kasagama's hopes of acquiring exclusive control of Toro's affairs could not be maintained against the encroaching forces of economic development. But Rukidi was shrewd enough to see that cooperation with the Protectorate authorities in the economic sphere might bring its rewards, in the shape of greater wealth and of immunity from interference in the basic exercise of power between king and people. All this scheming was to prove worthless, however, when Uganda became independent. A Protectorate Administration which could draw upon limitless power from overseas if the need arose could afford to connive at petty local tyrannies, especially when the subject people seemed to enjoy their subservience because it ministered to their local pride; especially, too, when local rulers took much of the burden of day-to-day administration from the shoulders of busy Protectorate officials. But an independent Government of Uganda, all too conscious of its inexperience and its limited resources, needed to demonstrate its sovereignty if it were to make a success of running the country.

The majority of the people of Uganda, like the inhabitants of every other newly independent African country, knew nothing of patriotism, or even of nationalism, beyond the confines of their tribal units. Unlike many of those other countries, Uganda had no single charismatic leader to provide a focus for incipient nationalist sentiments. The loyalty of the Baganda to their Kabaka and of the majority of the inhabitants of the western kingdoms to their own rulers showed the nature of their ideas of leadership. But in the kingdoms the spread of western-style education had awakened ideas of democracy, even if in some areas they were quickly stifled by the power of the traditional ruler, or else were hidden secretly away lest they brought those who believed in them into disrepute with the ancient authorities. The Legislative Council, too, under Cohen's skilled guidance, had provided an important training-ground in democratic procedures. But if it was democracy which undermined the kingdoms, it was the sovereign power of the Uganda Government which toppled them. In the struggle for authority the lesser power of 'traditional' Toro was swept away by the greater power of the new Uganda.

Upon these developments the people of Toro as a whole had exerted little positive influence. Their role had been for the most part a quiescent one. Unlike the Baganda they had not rallied in strength to resist the changes which seemed to threaten their way of life. Their attachment to the monarchy was less emotional. For many the ruling families still seemed alien, and their affection for Rukidi was for the man rather than for what he represented. On the other hand Toro was not a seething centre of political activity. Uganda's achievement of independence was not in any case the result of a mass movement. It was the work of an elite, aided and encouraged, particularly in Cohen's time, by a few able officials. Tribal divisions, as Obote frequently regretted, both restricted the opportunities for popular action and encouraged local rather than national loyalties. In Toro, perhaps more than in some districts, the people had come to accept what each day gave, not in a sullen, resentful fashion, nor yet with lack-lustre resignation, but philosophically, as men who have seen many changes and will see many more, but who have the satisfaction of living in a beautiful and fertile land.

Notes

INTRODUCTION

1. S. R. Karugire, *A History of the Kingdom of Nkore in Western Uganda to 1896*, p. 125.
2. M. S. M. Kiwanuka, *A History of Buganda from the Foundation of the Kingdom to 1900*, pp. 39–40.
3. Karugire, p. 120.
4. Kiwanuka, p. 46.
5. R. Oliver, 'Discernible Developments in the Interior c. 1500–1800', in R. Oliver and G. Mathew (eds.), *History of East Africa*, Vol. I, pp. 180–2; B. A. Ogot, *A History of the Southern Luo*, Vol. I, p. 46; Karugire, p. 125.
6. Kiwanuka, pp. 46–63.
7. Kasagama, *Memoir* (this typewritten version is almost certainly a copy of an MS. translation prepared at Makerere University under the direction of Mr O. W. Furley which was subsequently lost, see *Uganda Journal*, Vol. XXXI, No. 2, 1967, p. 183); and oral communication from Mr J. Kaboha.
8. K.W., 'The Kings of Bunyoro-Kitara', Pt. II, *Uganda Journal*, Vol. IV, pp. 75–6. This three-part narrative appeared in the *Uganda Journal* as follows: Pt. I–Vol. III, No. 2, 1935, pp. 155–60; Pt. II–Vol. IV, No. 1, 1936, pp. 75–83; Pt. III–Vol. V, No. 1, 1937, pp. 53–67.
9. J. Beattie, *The Nyoro State*, pp. 60–1.
10. K. Ingham, 'The Amagasani of the Abakama of Bunyoro', pp. 138–45.
11. Beattie, p. 129.
12. J. H. Speke, *Journal of the Discovery of the Source of the Nile*, pp. 573, 576.
13. E. C. Lanning, 'Notes on the History of Koki', pp. 162–3.
14. K.W., 'The Kings of Bunyoro-Kitara', *Uganda Journal*, Vol. IV, p. 79.
15. J. Tosh, 'The Northern Interlacustrine Region', in J. R. Gray and D. B. Birmingham (eds.), *Pre-Colonial African Trade*, p. 104.

16. Speke, p. 509.
17. D. A. Low, 'The Northern Interior', in Oliver and Mathew (eds.), *History of East Africa*, p. 327.
18. J. A. Grant, *A Walk Across Africa*, p. 293.
19. E. R. Kamuhangire, 'Pre-Colonial Trade in south-western Uganda'.

CHAPTER I

1. Because Toro was an offshoot of Bunyoro-Kitara much of the written information about the kingdom comes from Kinyoro sources. The histories of the rulers of Bunyoro by K.W. (c.f. Introduction, note 8), by J. W. Nyakatura (*Abakama ba Bunyoro Kitara*), P. Bikunya (*Ky 'Abakama ba Bunyoro*), and H. K. Karubanga (*Bukya Nibwira*), all contain useful evidence which in some cases can be checked by reference to Sir Apolo Kaggwa, *The Kings of Buganda*, and to the work of such recent historians as Kiwanuka and Karugire. Of interest, too, is Mrs A. B. Fisher's *Twilight Tales of the Black Baganda*, much of which was based upon information given by Mukama Duhaga IV of Bunyoro. Kasagama's *Memoir* was itself based upon the Mukama's recollections of information passed on to him orally and upon his personal experiences as ruler of Toro. It appears to be both a frank and accurate record.
2. K. Ingham, 'The Amagasani of the Abakama of Bunyoro', p. 138.
3. K.W., 'The Kings of Bunyoro-Kitara', *Uganda Journal*, Vol. V, p. 60.
4. Bikunya, pp. 53, 66; Beattie, pp. 113–14; Nyakatura, pp. 265–6.
5. Nyakatura, p. 121.
6. *ibid.*, p. 119.
7. Fisher, pp. 147–9.
8. Kasagama, *Memoir*.
9. K.W., 'The Kings of Bunyoro-Kitara', *Uganda Journal*, Vol. V, p. 60.
10. Fisher, p. 150.
11. *ibid.*
12. Bikunya, p. 66.
13. Karubanga, p. 13.
14. K.W., 'The Kings of Bunyoro-Kitara', *Uganda Journal*, Vol. V, p. 60.

15. *ibid.*, p. 61.
16. S. W. Baker, *Albert Nyanza*, Vol. I, pp. 251, 348–50; Vol. II, p. 138.
17. *ibid.*, Vol. II, p. 101.
18. c.f. Speke, p. 405 for an account of the reception of an army which had been victorious in a campaign against Busoga, and Baker, *Albert Nyanza*, Vol. II, pp. 213, 240 for an account of attacks upon Bunyoro.
19. Baker, *Albert Nyanza*, Vol. II, p. 24.
20. *ibid.*, pp. 192–7.
21. *ibid.*
22. Oral communication from the late Mugema of Bunyoro to the author, 1951.
23. Kaggwa, p. 160.

CHAPTER II

1. Karugire, p. 218.
2. *ibid.*, pp. 181–9.
3. *ibid.*, pp. 220–1.
4. H. M. Stanley, *In Darkest Africa*, pp. 511–12.
5. Karugire, pp. 214–17; K.W., 'The Kings of Bunyoro-Kitara', *Uganda Journal*, Vol. V, p. 63; Fisher, p. 161.
6. Kasagama, *Memoir*; Kaggwa, p. 160.
7. H. M. Stanley, *Through the Dark Continent*, p. 301. Stanley refers to Toro as Gambaragara.
8. Kaggwa, p. 160; Stanley, *Through the Dark Continent*, p. 301.
9. S. W. Baker, *Ismailia*, New edn 1890, pp. 337, 362–6, 376–9, 401, 405.
10. *ibid.*, p. 432.
11. *ibid.*, p. 451.
12. Low, 'The Northern Interior', pp. 343–4.
13. Sir John Milner Gray, 'The Diaries of Emin Pasha', p. 161, entry for 16 Sept. 1877.
14. Fisher, p. 167.
15. Kasagama, *Memoir*.
16. Bikunya, p. 66.
17. Stanley, *Through the Dark Continent*, pp. 270–1.
18. Fisher, pp. 167–8.
19. *ibid.*
20. *ibid.*
21. Nyakatura, p. 157.

22. Kasagama, *Memoir.*
23. Kaggwa, p. 167; Kasagama, *Memoir.*
24. Stanley, *Through the Dark Continent,* p. 271.
25. Kasagama, *Memoir*; Kaggwa, p. 178.
26. Bikunya, p. 66.
27. Stanley, *In Darkest Africa,* p. 456.
28. For a more detailed description of the formation, structure and operation of Kabarega's military system see G. M. Uzoigwe, *Revolution and Revolt in Bunyoro-Kitara.*
29. Stanley, *In Darkest Africa,* p. 456.
30. Karugire, pp. 218, 223–4.
31. Stanley, *In Darkest Africa,* pp. 510–11.
32. *ibid.*, pp. 509–10, 521.

CHAPTER III

1. E. Hertslet, *The Map of Africa by Treaty,* Vol. I, pp. 345 ff.
2. S. E. Crowe, *The Berlin West Africa Conference, 1884–85,* pp. 176–91; C. H. Alexandrowicz, 'The Partition of Africa by Treaty', in K. Ingham (ed.), *Foreign Relations of African States,* pp. 229–55.
3. Draft reply of the Marquis of Salisbury to Count H. Hatzfeldt, August 1887, F.O. Confidential Print 5736.
4. H. Jenkyns and C. P. Ilbert, Memorandum on the Draft Jurisdiction Bill, 18 June 1888; R. S. Wright, Memorandum on the Foreign Jurisdiction Bill, 15 Nov. 1888; H. Jenkyns' reply to R. S. Wright's Memorandum, 16 Nov. 1888; R. S. Wright, Note 'B', 22 Nov. 1888; H. Jenkyns' remarks on Note 'B', 22 Nov. 1888. F.O. 97/562. For drawing my attention to this exchange of views regarding the foreign jurisdiction of the Crown I am indebted to Dr A. F. Madden of Nuffield College, Oxford.
5. Margery Perham (ed.), *Diaries of Lord Lugard,* Vol. II, p. 181.
6. *ibid.*, p. 168.
7. *ibid.*, pp. 168–70.
8. *ibid.*, p. 201.
9. *ibid.*, p. 227.
10. *ibid.*, p. 268.
11. *ibid.*, pp. 287–8.
12. *ibid.*, p. 303.
13. *ibid.*, p. 314.
14. *ibid.*, p. 370.
15. *ibid.*, pp. 366–7, 374, 393, 397–8.

16. *ibid.*, p. 376.
17. *ibid.*, pp. 373–88.
18. *ibid.*, pp. 407–12.
19. *ibid.*, pp. 420, 425.
20. Kasagama, *Memoir*.
21. Perham, Vol. II, p. 48.
22. *ibid.*, Vol. III, pp. 117–18.
23. *ibid.*, pp. 148–50.
24. *Papers relating to Uganda*. Africa, No. 7, 1895. *C. 7708*, p. 73.
25. W. E. Hall, *op. cit.*, p. 221.
26. H. F. Morris and J. S. Reid, *Indirect Rule and the Search for Justice*, p. 48.
27. O. W. Furley, 'The Reign of Kasagama in Toro from a Contemporary Account', p. 186.
28. Hertslet, Vol. I, p. 397.
29. Kasagama, *Memoir*.
30. R. Baile to Sir Harry Johnston, Fort Portal, 19 Oct. 1900. Uganda National Archives (henceforward U.N.A.) File A.14, Item I.
31. H.M. Special Commissioner to R. Baile, Entebbe, 19 Dec. 1900. U.N.A. File A.14, Item III.
32. R. Baile to Sir Harry Johnston, Fort Portal, 16 Jan. 1901. U.N.A. File A.14, Item I.
33. Kasagama, *Memoir*.
34. Salisbury to Ternan, 29 Sept. 1899 F.O. 2/200.

CHAPTER IV

1. Kasagama, *Memoir*.
2. Maddox to Wilson, Kabarole, 3 Sept. 1900, Enclosure in Wilson to Elgin, 22 Jan. 1906. C.O. 536/5.
3. I. H. B. Stanford, 'Historical and Political Notes on Toro District', written for the first visit to Toro of the Governor, Sir Bernard Bourdillon, in 1933. Unpublished.
4. Wilson to Collectors, Western Province, Masinde, 10 Oct. 1900. U.N.A. File A.15, Item I.
5. C.M.S., *Extracts from the Annual Letters of the Missionaries*, 1903, p. 237.
6. Report by George Wilson on the murder of Harry Galt, enclosed in letter from Sir James Hayes Sadler to Colonial Secretary, 25 Aug. 1905, C.O. 536/2.
7. Numerous letters between the Sub-Commissioner Western Pro-

vince and the Sub-Commissioner Kampala from 28 April 1903 to 26 Oct. 1903. U.N.A. File A.12, Item IV.
8. S. Ormsby to Sub-Commissioner Western Province, Fort Portal, 8 Dec. 1902. U.N.A. File A.12, Item II.
9. J. P. Wilson to H.M. Commissioner and Consul General, Fort Portal, 31 Dec. 1902. U.N.A. File A.12, Item II.
10. J. P. Wilson to H.M. Commissioner and Consul General, Fort Portal, 9 Jan. 1903. U.N.A. File A.12, Item III.
11. Minute of *baraza* held in Fort Portal, 9 Feb. 1903. U.N.A. File A.14, Item III.
12. S. Ormsby, Monthly Report on Toro District for Feb. 1903, Fort Portal, 10 March 1903. U.N.A. File A.12, Item III.
13. J. A. Haldane to District Commissioner Toro, Mbarara, 4 Oct. 1911. U.N.A. Secretariat Minute Paper 1235.
14. J. A. Haldane, Reports on Toro District for Jan. and March 1905, U.N.A. File A.14, Item II.
15. *Church Missionary Intelligencer for 1897*, p. 787, and *for 1899*, p. 103.
16. S. Bagge to H.M. Commissioner and Consul General, Hoima, 13 Feb. U.N.A. File A.12, Item II; *C.M. Intelligencer for 1904*, p. 529.
17. Sadler to Colonial Secretary, May 1905. C.O. 536/1.
18. *C.M. Intelligencer for 1900*, p. 218.
19. *C.M. Intelligencer for 1901*, p. 239.
20. *C.M. Intelligencer for 1903*, p. 183.
21. Everard G. M. Wylde, Report on Toro District for Oct. 1901, Fort Portal, 4 Nov. 1901. U.N.A. File A.14, Item I.
22. S. Ormsby to Sub-Commissioner Western Province, Fort Portal, 8 Dec. 1902. U.N.A. File A.12, Item II.
23. J. P. Wilson to H.M. Commissioner and Consul General, 9 Jan. 1903. U.N.A. File A.12, Item III.
24. J. Hayes Sadler, Memorandum to Sub-Commissioner Western Province, Entebbe, 11 March 1904. U.N.A. File A.12, Item IV.
25. J. H. G. McDougall, Annual Report on Toro District for 1911–12, Fort Portal, 20 May 1912. U.N.A. File A.15, Item II; SMP 632B.
26. George Wilson to Elgin, 21 April 1906. C.O. 536/6.
27. Sadler, Memorandum to Sub-Commissioner Western Province, 11 March 1904, U.N.A. File A.12, Item IV.
28. J. P. Wilson, Report on Western Province for March 1903, Fort Portal. U.N.A. File A.12, Item III.
29. J. P. Wilson to H.M. Commissioner and Consul General, Fort Portal, 20 June 1903, U.N.A. File A.12, Item III.

30. Galt to Acting Commissioner, Fort Portal, 1 May 1905. U.N.A. File A.14, Item II.
31. Petition of Toro Lukiko, 8 Jan. 1906. U.N.A. File A.14, Item III.
32. Elgin to Bell, 15 and 20 June 1906. C.O. 536/6.
33. Uganda Protectorate, *Inquiry into the Grievances of the Mukama and People of Toro*, p. 19, Appendix C.
34. Kasagama, *Memoir*.
35. L. H. Cubitt, Annual Report on Toro District for 1910–11: U.N.A. File A.15, Item I, SMP 632A; J. H. G. McDougall, Annual Report on Toro District for 1911–12: U.N.A. File A.15, Item II, SMP 632B.
36. Tarrant to J. F. Cunningham, 3 March 1901. U.N.A. File A.14, Item I.
37. S. Ormsby to Sub-Commissioner Western Province, 3 Jan. 1903. U.N.A. File A.12, Item III.
38. Wilson to Sadler, 30 July 1905, enclosed in Sadler to Colonial Secretary, 24 Aug. 1905. C.O. 536/2.
39. O. W. Furley, 'Kasagama of Toro', p. 192.
40. Stephen S. Bagge to H.M. Commissioner and Consul General, Hoima, 9 Jan. 1902. U.N.A. File A.12, Item II.
41. Fisher to Tarrant, Kabarole, 21 April 1901. U.N.A. File A.14, Item I.
42. Bagge to H.M. Commissioner and Consul General, Hoima, 9 Jan. 1902. U.N.A. File A.12, Item II.
43. Baile to Johnston, Fort Portal, 11 Oct. 1900. U.N.A. File A.14, Item I.
44. S. Ormsby to Sub-Commissioner Western Province, Fort Portal, 2 Jan. 1903. U.N.A. File A.12, Item III.
45. J. H. G. McDougall, Annual Report on Toro District for 1911–12, Fort Portal, 20 May 1912. U.N.A. File A.15, Item II.
46. Toro Agreement (Judicial) 1912. U.N.A. File C.2, Item II.
47. Kasagama, *Memoir*.
48. Minute of Sir Robert Coryndon, undated. C.O. 536/139.
49. P. W. Cooper, Annual Report on Western Province for 1923. U.N.A. File A.15, Item II; SMP/632B.
50. Sir Geoffrey Archer, Minute, 2 Sept. 1923. C.O. 536/139.
51. Sir William Gowers to Colonial Secretary, 21 May 1926. C.O. 536/139.
52. Uganda Protectorate, *Report of the Committee of Inquiry into the Grievances of the Mukama and People of Toro, 1926*.
53. L. S. Amery to Governor of Uganda, 15 Jan. 1927. C.O. 536/143.

CHAPTER V

1. W. G. Adams, Report on the Western Province for 1931. U.N.A. File A.15, Item II.
2. Sir Philip Mitchell, 'Indirect Rule', pp. 101–7.
3. Uganda Protectorate, *Annual Report of the Education Department for 1939*, Government Printer, Entebbe, 1940, pp. 25, 31–3.
4. Uganda Protectorate, *Annual Report of the Medical Department for 1939*, Government Printer, Entebbe, 1940, p. 42.
5. Uganda Protectorate, *Annual Report on the Kingdom of Buganda, Eastern Province and Western Province for 1939–1946*, Government Printer, Entebbe, 1949, pp. 66, 69–72, 85, 89, 91–2, 99, 101.
6. C. A. G. Wallis, *Report of an Inquiry into African Local Government in the Protectorate of Uganda*, Government Printer, Entebbe, 1953.
7. Uganda Protectorate, *Proceedings of the Legislative Council*, 13 April 1954, p. 24.
8. *ibid.*, 11 Jan. 1956, p. 51.
9. Uganda Protectorate, *Elections to Legislative Council*, Sessional Paper No. 4 of 1957/58, Government Printer, Entebbe, 1957.
10. Uganda Protectorate, *Proceedings of the Legislative Council*, 29 April 1957, pp. 19–33.
11. *ibid.*, 7 Aug. 1957, p. 19.
12. *ibid.*, 30 Sept. 1957, pp. 26–9.
13. *ibid.*, 26 Sept. 1958, p. 145.
14. D. A. Low, *Political Parties in Uganda*, p. 30.
15. Uganda Protectorate, *Report of the Constitutional Committee 1959*, Government Printer, Entebbe, 1959.

CHAPTER VI

1. Memorandum from the Buganda *Lukiiko* for submission to Her Majesty the Queen being the desire of the Baganda to bring the Buganda Treaty of 1894 to an end, 16 Dec. 1958.
2. Uganda Protectorate, *Proceedings of the Legislative Council*, 23 Sept. 1960, p. 1549; 28 Sept. 1960, p. 1653.
3. Uganda Protectorate, *Report of the Relationships Commission 1961*, Government Printer, Entebbe, 1961, p. 23.
4. *ibid.*
5. *ibid.*, pp. 43–51.
6. *Uganda Argus*, 19 March 1962.
7. *ibid.*, 2 April 1962.

8. *ibid.*, 7 Aug. 1962; 13 Aug. 1962.
9. F. A. Knowles to Chief Secretary, Mubende, 1 Sept. 1909, U.N.A. SMP 1313.
10. *Uganda Argus*, 10 April 1967.
11. *ibid.*, 19 June 1967.

Bibliography

UNPUBLISHED SOURCES

Public Record Office
The following files are useful:

F.O. 2/200	C.O. 536/15
F.O. 97/562	C.O. 536/39
C.O. 536/1	C.O. 536/43
C.O. 536/2	C.O. 536/50
C.O. 536/3	C.O. 536/53
C.O. 536/5	C.O. 536/59
C.O. 536/6	C.O. 536/139
C.O. 536/7	C.O. 536/143
C.O. 536/13	C.O. 682/4
C.O. 536/14	C.O. 682/8
	C.O. 691/83

Uganda National Archives, Entebbe
The following files are useful:

A.12, Items I, II, III, IV, V, VI, VII.
A.14, Items I, II, III.
A.15, Items I, II.
A.27, Item III.
SMP Nos. 157, 418, 632, 663, 931, 1019/06, 1235, 1251/091, 1251/0911, 1313/09, 1345, 1635, 2083, 2198, 2202, 2208, 2395, 2714, 2749/I, 3104, 3481, 3622, 4436, 7098.

Miscellaneous
Kasagama, *Memoir.*

PRINTED SOURCES

Parliamentary Papers
Papers relating to Uganda Africa No. 7, 1895, C. 7708.

Uganda Government Publications
Summary of the Proceedings of the Legislative Council, 1921–1939.

Proceedings of the Legislative Council, 1939–1962.
Annual Reports on the Western Province.
Annual Reports of the Medical Department.
Annual Reports of the Education Department.
Report of the Committee of Inquiry into the Grievances of the Mukama and People of Toro, 1926.
C. A. G. Wallis, *Report of an Inquiry into African Local Government in the Protectorate of Uganda*, 1953.
Elections to Legislative Council, Sessional Paper No. 4 of 1957/58.
Report of the Constitutional Committee 1959.
Report of the Relationships Commission 1961.

Church Missionary Society Publications
Church Missionary Intelligencer, 1895–1906.
Church Missionary Review, 1907–1927.
Extracts from the Annual Letters of the Missionaries, 1903–1912.
The Church Overseas, 1928–1934.

Newspapers
Uganda Argus, 1955–67.
Uganda Herald, 1912–55.

Books
Ashe, R. P. *Chronicles of Uganda*. Hodder, London, 1894.
—— *Two Kings of Uganda*. Sampson Low, London, 1890.
Askwith, G. R. and Bovill, Major. *Roddy Owen*. John Murray, London, 1897.
Baker, S. W. *Albert Nyanza*. Macmillan, London, 1866, 2 Vols.
—— *Ismailia*. Macmillan, London, 1874, new edn 1890.
Beattie, J. *The Nyoro State*. Clarendon Press, Oxford, 1971.
Bell, Sir Hesketh. *Glimpses of a Governor's Life*. Sampson Low, London, 1946.
Bikunya, P. *Ky'Abakama ba Bunyoro*. Sheldon Press, London, 1927.
Chaillé Long, C. *Central Africa*. Sampson Low, London, 1876.
—— *My Life in Four Continents*. Hutchinson, London, 1912, 2 Vols.
Colville, H. *The Land of the Nile Springs*. Arnold, London, 1895.
Crazzolara, Fr. J. P. *The Lwoo*. Museum Combonianum, Verona, Pt. I, 1950, P. II, 1951, Pt. III, 1954.
Crowe, S. E. *The Berlin West Africa Conference, 1884–85*. Longmans, Green & Co., London, 1942.
Fisher, Mrs A. B. *On the Borders of Pigmy-Land*. Marshall, London, undated.
—— *Twilight Tales of the Black Baganda*. Marshall, London, 1911.

Grant, J. A. *A Walk Across Africa*. Blackwood, Edinburgh and London, 1864.

Gray, J. R. and Birmingham, D. B. (eds.) *Pre-Colonial African Trade*. O.U.P., London, 1970.

Hall, W. E. *A Treatise on the Foreign Powers and Jurisdiction of the Crown*. Clarendon Press, Oxford, 1894.

Hertslet, E. *The Map of Africa by Treaty*. H.M.S.O., London, 3rd edn 1909, 3 vols.

Ibingira, G. S. K. *The Forging of an African Nation*. Viking Press, New York, 1973.

Ingham, K. *The Making of Modern Uganda*. Allen & Unwin, London, 1958.

—— (ed.) *Foreign Relations of African States*. Butterworth, London, 1974.

Johnson, T. B. *Tramps round the Mountains of the Moon*. T. Fisher Unwin, London, 1912.

Kaggwa, Sir Apolo. *The Kings of Buganda* (trans. M. S. M. Kiwanuka). East African Publishing House, Nairobi, 1971.

Karubanga, H. K. *Bukya Nibwira*. Eagle Press, East Africa, 1949.

Karugire, S. R. *A History of the Kingdom of Nkore in Western Uganda to 1896*. Clarendon Press, Oxford, 1971.

Kiwanuka, M. S. M. *A History of Buganda from the Foundation of the Kingdom to 1900*. Longmans, London, 1971.

Low, D. A. *Political Parties in Uganda*. Institute of Commonwealth Studies, Commonwealth Paper No. 8, Athlone Press, London, 1962.

Lugard, Lord. *The Rise of our East African Empire*. Blackwood, Edinburgh and London, 1893.

—— *The Dual Mandate in Tropical Africa*. Blackwood, Edinburgh and London, 1926.

Mitchell, Sir Philip. *African Afterthoughts*. Hutchinson, London, 1954.

Morris, H. F. and Reid, J. S. *Indirect Rule and the Search for Justice*. Clarendon Press, Oxford, 1972.

Nyakatura, J. W. *Abakama ba Bunyoro Kitara*. St Justin, P.Q., Canada, 1947.

Ogot, B. A. *A History of the Southern Luo*. East African Publishing House, Nairobi, Vol. I, 1967.

Oliver, R. *The Missionary Factor in East Africa*. Longmans, Green, London, 1952.

Oliver, R. and Mathew G. (eds.) *History of East Africa*. Clarendon Press, Oxford, Vol. I, 1963.

Perham, Margery (ed.) *Diaries of Lord Lugard.* Vols. 1, 2 and 3. Faber and Faber, London, 1959.
—— *Lugard, The Years of Adventure, 1858–1890.* Collins, London, 1956.
Portal, Sir G. *The British Mission to Uganda in 1893.* Arnold, London, 1894.
Pringle, M. A. *A Journey in East Africa towards the Mountains of the Moon.* Blackwood, Edinburgh and London, 1886.
Roscoe, J. *The Bakitara or Banyoro.* C.U.P., London, 1923.
Schweitzer, G. *The Life and Work of Emin Pasha.* Constable, London, 1898, 2 Vols.
Speke, J. H. *Journal of the Discovery of the Source of the Nile.* William Blackwood & Sons, Edinburgh and London, 1863.
Stacey, Tom. *Summons to Ruwenzori.* Secker & Warburg, London, 1965.
Stanley, H. M. *Through the Dark Continent.* Sampson Low, London, 18th edn 1879.
—— *In Darkest Africa.* Sampson Low, London, 1890.
Uzoigwe, G. M. *Revolution and Revolt in Bunyoro-Kitara.* Makerere History Papers No. 5, Kampala, 1970.

Articles

Bere, R. M. 'Outline of Acholi History', *Uganda Journal,* Vol. XI. No. 1, 1947.
Furley, O. W. 'Kasagama of Toro', *Uganda Journal,* Vol. XXV, No. 2, 1961.
—— 'The Reign of Kasagama in Toro from a Contemporary Account', *Uganda Journal,* Vol. XXXI, No. 2, 1967.
Gray, Sir John Milner. 'The Diaries of Emin Pasha', *Uganda Journal,* Vol. XXV, No. 2, 1961.
—— 'Toro in 1897', *Uganda Journal,* Vol. XVII, No. 1, 1953.
Ingham, K. 'The Amagasani of the Abakama of Bunyoro', *Uganda Journal,* Vol. XVII, No. 2, 1953.
Kamuhangire, E. R. 'Pre-Colonial Trade in South-western Uganda', *Makerere Seminar Papers* 28/71/72.
K.W. 'The Kings of Bunyoro-Kitara', *Uganda Journal,* Vol. III, No. 2, 1935; Vol. IV, No. 1, 1936; Vol. V, No. 1, 1937.
Lanning, E. C. 'Notes on the History of Koki', *Uganda Journal,* Vol. XXIII, No. 2, 1959.
Mitchell, Sir Philip. 'Indirect Rule', *Uganda Journal,* Vol. IV, No. 2, 1936.

Index

Printed in the United States
by Baker & Taylor Publisher Services